THE UL͏ BRITISH ROYAL NAVY QUIZ

B.R. EGGINTON

Contents

Prologue

'England expects that every man will do his duty.'
Horatio Nelson, 21 October 1805

The navy has always been an integral part of the English nation: from the darkest depths of the Middles Ages when England came into being, all the way to the present day.

After the Battle of Trafalgar in 1805 the Royal Navy became the undisputed master of the seas for over a century, laying the foundations for the largest empire the world has ever known. And even though its glory days have long since been and gone, the English people continue to feel a strong sense of attachment to their 'Senior Service'.

In short, the Royal Navy isn't just a means of security, it's a cultural institution – the beating heart of the crown and country it serves. And that's no exaggeration. Without the Royal Navy to keep shipping lanes safe for English merchants, it is doubtful that England would have achieved any of the things that make it great: the steam engine, the jet engine, the telegraph, the chocolate bar, the incandescent light bulb, the lawnmower, the power loom, the tank and even the World Wide Web.

This book is divided into four sections – General, People, Battles and Ships – and so whatever your area of interest (or ability) there is something in this book for you!

No matter how much you think you know about the Royal Navy, there's always plenty more to learn about the service's most glorious triumphs and also, more importantly, its most ignominious defeats – for it is through failure that the individual (and in turn the nation) improves.

General

General 1 (easy)

Q1 Who said: 'There must be a beginning of any great matter, but the continuing unto the end until it be thoroughly finished yields the true glory'?

A Cuthbert Collingwood
B Henry VIII
C Francis Drake
D Horatio Nelson

Q2 What ship did Charles Darwin famously sail on?

A HMS *Beagle*
B *Golden Hind*
C HMS *Prince of Wales*
D HMS *Ark Royal*

Q3 How many ports does the term 'Cinque Ports' refer to?

A 1
B 3
C 5
D 7

Q4 The poem *Libelle of Englyshe Polycye* was composed after a siege on what port?

A Roscoff
B Plymouth
C Calais
D Dover

Q5 The sailor Edward Barlow is best remembered for what?

A Sacrificing himself to save the rest of his crew
B Setting fire to his ship
C Plotting to kill Henry VIII
D His journal

Q6 Richard Nicolls was the first colonial governor of what?

A Canada
B New York
C Hong Kong
D India

Q7 In what year was the Longitude Act passed?

A 1512
B 1600
C 1714
D 1901

Q8 Who wrote the lyrics for *Rule, Britannia!*?

A James Thomson
B Lord Byron
C C. S. Forester
D Thomas Arne

Q9 *Teredo navalis* are better known by what name?

A Ship maggots
B Ship cats
C Ship lice
D Ship worm

Q10 The salted meat consumed on board sailing ships was known by what other name?

A Salt slop
B Salt heaven
C Salt junk
D Salt fluid

General 2 (easy)

Q1 What was Gilbert Blane's occupation?

A Physician
B Politician
C Admiral
D Tailor

Q2 What writer created the fictional character Horatio Hornblower?

A Charles Dickens
B Rudyard Kipling
C Mark Twain
D C. S. Forester

Q3 What naval squadron was formed after the Slave Trade Act of 1807 was passed?

A South Pacific Squadron
B Atlantic Squadron
C North Sea Squadron
D West African Squadron

Q4 In what year was the Royal Naval Reserve created?

A 1649
B 1790
C 1859
D 1914

Q5 The Naval Defence Act 1889 formally adopted what?

A Two-power standard
B Navy entrance tests
C Blockade of Germany
D Steamships

Q6 What room was the cryptanalysis section of the British Admiralty based in during the First World War?

A 1
B 40
C 55
D 101

Q7 How many countries signed the London Naval Treaty (1930)?

A 2
B 4
C 5
D 12

Q8 What class of submarine was introduced to the Royal Navy in 1994?

A Vanguard class
B Illustrious class
C Nelson class
D Destroyer class

Q9 What is the second highest rank in the Royal Navy?

A Commodore
B Rear Admiral
C Admiral
D Commander

Q10 As of 2019, when was the most recent Royal Navy fleet review held?

A 1945
B 1982
C 2005
D 2011

General 3 (easy)

Q1 What was the occupation of Patrick O'Brian?

A Merchant sailor
B Author
C Naval officer
D Physician

Q2 The Royal Navy is referred to as the what?

A Senior Service
B Superior Service
C Seafaring Service
D Stellar Service

Q3 What is the official march of the Royal Navy?

A *Hearts of Lions*
B *Heart of St George*
C *Heart of Oak*
D *Hearts of Courage*

Q4 How many commissioned ships did the Royal Navy have in 2018?

A 32
B 74
C 90
D 112

Q5 *HMS Holland 1* was the first what commissioned by the Royal Navy?

A Reconnaissance plane
B Aircraft carrier
C Battleship
D Submarine

Q6 Type 23 frigates are known by what other name?

A King class
B Duke class
C Queen class
D Earl class

Q7 What is the highest rank in the Royal Navy?

A First Lord of the Admiralty
B Admiral of the Fleet
C Commander of the Fleet
D Rear Admiral

Q8 What name is commonly used to refer to English seamen?

A Jack Tar
B Tommy
C Marine
D Britannia's Best

Q9 Covey Crump compiled a record of what?

A Naval slang
B High-ranking officers
C Royal Navy ships
D Deaths in battle

Q10 What was the Royal Navy's first nuclear-powered submarine?

A HMS *Britannia*
B HMS *Invincible*
C HMS *Submerged*
D HMS *Dreadnought*

General 4 (easy)

Q1 What is the oldest commissioned ship in the Royal Navy?

A HMS *Ark Royal*
B HMS *Victory*
C HMS *Endeavour*
D HMS *Hermes*

Q2 AgustaWestland AW159 Wildcat is a type of what?

A Car
B Ship
C Plane
D Helicopter

Q3 What is the Royal Navy flag called?

A Navy Cross
B Jolly Roger
C White Ensign
D Union Jack

Q4 In what year was the first submarine commissioned in the Royal Navy?

A 1889
B 1901
C 1912
D 1923

Q5 The Britannia Royal Naval College is located in what English county?

A Merseyside
B Cornwall
C Wiltshire
D Devon

Q6 As of 2019 what is the name of the Royal Navy's only ice patrol ship?

A HMS *Explorer*
B HMS *Endurance*
C HMS *Hercules*
D HMS *Protector*

Q7 How many fighting arms are there to the Royal Navy?

A 1
B 3
C 5
D 9

Q8 The F-35 Lightning II are produced in what country?

A India
B Germany
C Canada
D USA

Q9 What is Uckers?

A Royal Navy mascot
B Song
C Fitness routine
D Board game

Q10 The Submarine Command Course was created during what war?

A First World War
B Second World War
C Korean War
D Falklands War

General 5 (easy)

Q1 How many bases does the Royal Navy have in the United Kingdom?

A 1
B 3
C 6
D 17

Q2 The largest navy base in Western Europe is located near what city?

A Plymouth
B Belfast
C Liverpool
D Southampton

Q3 In what city is the HMS *Victory* kept in a dry dock?

A Liverpool
B Portsmouth
C Southampton
D London

Q4 The Bombardment of Algiers was an attempt by the Royal Navy to suppress what?

A Piracy
B Slavery
C Colonists
D Smuggling

Q5 What was the first iron-hulled, armour-plated warship?

A HMS *Hermes*
B HMS *Devastation*
C HMS *Warrior*
D HMS *Ajax*

Q6 What country's fleet was famously scuttled at Scapa Flow?

A Germany
B France
C Spain
D Netherlands

Q7 What is the most junior officer rank in the Royal Navy?

A Midshipman
B Lieutenant
C Captain
D Major

Q8 The International Fleet Review 2005 was held to commemorate what battle?

A Battle of Jutland
B Battle of the Nile
C Battle of Trafalgar
D Battle of the Saintes

Q9 The term 'Cinque Ports' derives from what language?

A Latin
B French
C Norman French
D Dutch

Q10 What port remained in English hands until the reign of Mary I?

A Nice
B Sebastopol
C Saint-Malo
D Calais

General 6 (average)

Q1 What is the Royal Navy part of?

Q2 What king controversially tried to raise ship money during peacetime?

Q3 Who is the professional head of the Royal Navy?

Q4 The Royal Navy is part of what government department?

Q5 In what English counties are the Cinque Ports located?

Q6 The British Royal Navy was preceded by what two navies?

Q7 What Royal Navy officer famously sent the signal 'England expects that every man will do his duty'?

Q8 The oldest dry dock still in use, commissioned in 1495, is located in what city?

Q9 The Battle of Cape Spartel was part of what war?

Q10 The Northern Patrol took part in what two wars?

General 7 (average)

Q1 As of 2019, who is the Lord High Admiral?

Q2 What mutiny took place in September 1931?

Q3 Exercise Tiger was a rehearsal for what?

Q4 What branch of the Royal Navy was established in 1664?

Q5 What king commissioned the oldest dry dock still in use as of 2019?

Q6 A man o' war is an English expression for what?

Q7 What barge was commissioned to celebrate Elizabeth II's Diamond Jubilee?

Q8 What navy did the rebels form in the American Revolution?

Q9 The Cod Wars were fought between the United Kingdom and what other country?

Q10 The ARA *General Belgrano* was sunk during what war?

General 8 (average)

Q1 As of June 2019, who is the First Sea Lord?

Q2 A Jackstaff is a small vertical pole on the bow of a ship for what?

Q3 What youth organisation did the Admiralty sponsor in 1901?

Q4 Who wrote the *Aubrey–Maturin* series of novels?

Q5 What position was Nicholas Hine appointed to in 2019?

Q6 Where are the Royal Navy's main offices based?

Q7 What royal yacht was decommissioned in 1997?

Q8 What Scottish city was burned by a sea-borne army in 1544?

Q9 The Royal Navy was the largest navy in the world until part way through what war?

Q10 What shipping company owned the HMHS *Britannic*?

General 9 (average)

Q1 What does the Royal Navy motto *'Si vis pacem, para bellum'* mean?

Q2 Who became Fleet Commander in 2019?

Q3 As of 2019, how many royal yachts are in service?

Q4 How many Anglo-Dutch Wars were there?

Q5 The Battle of Santa Cruz de Tenerife was fought during what war?

Q6 What were the Dunkirkers?

Q7 Chatham Dockyard was located on what river?

Q8 How many colours are there on the Royal Navy flag?

Q9 What centuries did the Age of Sail cover?

Q10 How many Opium Wars did the Royal Navy take part in?

General 10 (average)

Q1 What class of aircraft carrier was the HMS *Illustrious*?

Q2 John Brown & Company was based in what town?

Q3 What type of letter gave a government licence for privateers to attack and capture vessels belonging to hostile nations?

Q4 The English Armada was assembled during whose reign?

Q5 Barbary pirates operated from the northern part of what continent?

Q6 Most of Denmark's navy was destroyed by the Royal Navy in what 1801 battle?

Q7 Who was Prime Minister when Horatio Nelson died?

Q8 What term refers to the forced recruitment of sailors into the navy?

Q9 What was the Royal Navy's main fleet during the First World War?

Q10 After the introduction of Dreadnought battleships, what were all earlier battleships called?

General 11 (expert)

Q1 Name the United Kingdom's three Royal Navy bases.

Q2 Name the five Cinque Ports.

Q3 What countries signed the London Naval Treaty (1930)?

Q4 What parliament passed the Navigation Act 1651?

Q5 A sailing ship in the Royal Navy needed to be at least what rate to be classified as a ship of the line?

Q6 What board, formed in the 17th century was responsible for medical services in the Royal Navy?

Q7 The Dover Patrol is notable for its involvement in what First World War raid?

Q8 In what years did the Royal Naval Air Service exist as an independent entity?

Q9 The Action of 11th November 2008 was a naval engagement against what group?

Q10 In what year did the Joint Expeditionary Force become active?

General 12 (expert)

Q1 What company built HMY *Britannia*?

Q2 After being captured by the English in the 15th century, what was the *Santa Clara* renamed?

Q3 The ship of the line was designed for what naval tactic?

Q4 What French ship was captured by the Royal Navy on its maiden voyage in 1798?

Q5 In what year did the Blockade of Africa begin?

Q6 In what year did the Fleet Air Arm become part of the Royal Navy?

Q7 In what year was the Women's Royal Naval Service established?

Q8 Who served as the First Sea Lord between 2006 and 2009?

Q9 What engine does the Westland Sea King have?

Q10 The Special Boat Service originates from what war?

General 13 (expert)

Q1 In what year was the HMY *Britannia* commissioned?

Q2 In what year did the Spithead and Nore mutinies occur?

Q3 What type of ship was *Great Michael*?

Q4 What class of battlecruiser was HMS *Repulse* (1916)?

Q5 In what year was the German battleship *Bismarck* sunk?

Q6 The Town-class are what kind of battleship?

Q7 In what year was the British Aerospace Sea Harrier introduced?

Q8 What Royal Navy ship took part in the Action of 11th November 2008?

Q9 How many Queen Elizabeth class aircraft carriers have been built?

Q10 The HMS *Raleigh* basic training facility is based in what town?

General 14 (expert)

Q1 What navy did *Margaret* belong to?

Q2 In what war did the United Kingdom capture Gibraltar?

Q3 What three countries were allies of the United Kingdom in the War of the Quadruple Alliance?

Q4 As of 2019, what is the Royal Navy's flagship?

Q5 In what year was the Second London Naval Treaty signed?

Q6 What Defence Secretary was controversially sacked in 2019?

Q7 Who served as Lord High Admiral between 1964 and 2011?

Q8 What commission was responsible for the day-to-day civil administration of the Royal Navy between 1546 and 1832?

Q9 The radio sitcom *The Navy Lark* featured what fictitious Royal Navy ship?

Q10 Who set *Rule, Britannia!* to music?

General 15 (expert)

Q1 What was the motto of the Royal Scots Navy?

Q2 The Royal Navy's rating system for sailing ships contained how many rates?

Q3 Gibraltar was ceded to the United Kingdom in what 1713 treaty?

Q4 Who is commander-in-chief of the armed forces?

Q5 Who designed the main Ministry of Defence building in Whitehall?

Q6 Where is Navy Command based?

Q7 HMS *Excellent* is what kind of frigate?

Q8 What is the only resident seagoing Royal Naval unit in Gibraltar?

Q9 Royal Navy ships are identified by what type of number?

Q10 In *Pirates of the Caribbean: The Curse of the Black Pearl* what is the fastest ship in the Royal Navy called?

People

Horatio Nelson

Q1 Horatio Nelson was killed during what battle?

Q2 Horatio Nelson was born and raised in what English county?

Q3 At what rank did Horatio Nelson enter the Royal Navy?

Q4 What was Horatio Nelson's favourite Royal Navy ship?

Q5 What was the occupation of Horatio Nelson's father, Edmund Nelson?

Q6 How was Maurice Suckling related to Horatio Nelson?

Q7 What body part did Horatio Nelson lose at the Battle of Santa Cruz de Tenerife?

Q8 Nelson's Column is situated in what London square?

Q9 Where is Horatio Nelson buried?

Q10 What major battle did Horatio Nelson win against the French in August 1798?

James Cook

Q1 James Cook produced detailed maps of what Canadian island?

Q2 James Cook died in what present-day US state?

Q3 James Cook was the first person to circumnavigate what island nation?

Q4 James Cook sailed on what ship on his first voyage of discovery?

Q5 How many voyages did James Cook lead?

Q6 What chief did James Cook attempt to kidnap shortly before his death?

Q7 In what year was James Cook killed?

Q8 James's Cook's first voyage was a combined expedition, financed by the Royal Navy and what society?

Q9 Who was James Cook's wife?

Q10 Makahiki is a festival held in honour of what god?

Harry Paye

Q1 In what century did Harry Paye die?

Q2 What was Harry Paye's occupation?

Q3 Harry Paye helped to suppress a Welsh revolt led by who?

Q4 What town was Harry Paye from?

Q5 Who wrote the children's novel *Arripay*, based on Harry Paye's life?

Q6 Where is the annual Harry Paye Charity Fun Day held?

Q7 Harry Paye mainly led raids against what two countries?

Q8 What did Harry Paye do to the city of Gijon?

Q9 What relation of Harry Paye was killed during a raid on his hometown?

Q10 Harry Paye was buried in what English county?

Charles Forbes

Q1 Charles Forbes served as commander-in-chief of what fleet during the Second World War?

Q2 What aircraft carrier was sunk on 8th June 1940?

Q3 What position was Charles Forbes appointed to in May 1941?

Q4 Charles Forbes retired during what war?

Q5 What First World War campaign did Charles Forbes take part in?

Q6 What hospital did Charles Forbes die in?

Q7 What military campaign did Charles Forbes take part in in 1940?

Q8 What military honour did Charles Forbes receive from France?

Q9 What training ship did Charles Forbes join in 1894?

Q10 Charles Forbes served as whose flag commander during the First World War?

George Rodney

Q1 George Rodney is best known for his victory in what 1782 battle?

Q2 How old was George Rodney when he joined the Royal Navy?

Q3 What territory did George Rodney famously seize in 1762?

Q4 George Rodney successfully resupplied Gibraltar after what 1780 battle?

Q5 What boarding school did George Rodney attend?

Q6 What was the first ship George Rodney served on?

Q7 What was George Rodney's middle name?

Q8 The Capture of Sint Eustatius occurred during what war?

Q9 What nickname was given to the Battle of Cape St Vincent?

Q10 Why did George Rodney flee to Paris in the 1770s?

Edward Hawke

Q1 Edward Hawke was captain of what ship during the Battle of Toulon?

Q2 Edward Hawke led the Royal Navy to victory in what key 1759 battle?

Q3 What French admiral did Edward Hawke face at the Second Battle of Cape Finisterre?

Q4 In what year did the Battle of Toulon take place?

Q5 Where was the Western Squadron based?

Q6 What position was Edward Hawke appointed to in 1766?

Q7 In what year was Edward Hawke first elected as a Member of Parliament?

Q8 What was the occupation of Edward Hawke's father?

Q9 Where did Edward Hawke die?

Q10 What rank was Edward Hawke promoted to in 1725?

Francis Drake

Q1 What monarch did Francis Drake serve?

Q2 What name was given to the area of present-day California that Francis Drake claimed for England?

Q3 What ship is Francis Drake most commonly associated with?

Q4 What title did Francis Drake hold in battle against the Spanish Armada?

Q5 In what present-day country did Francis Drake die?

Q6 Francis Drake was born in what English county?

Q7 What co-commander did Francis Drake have beheaded in 1578?

Q8 Francis Drake was the second person to do what?

Q9 In what year did Francis Drake receive a knighthood?

Q10 What manor house did Francis Drake purchase in 1580?

Thomas Mathews

Q1 What rank did Thomas Mathews reach in the Royal Navy?

Q2 How was Francis Wheler related to Thomas Mathews?

Q3 In what year did Thomas Mathews join the Royal Navy?

Q4 What country was Thomas Mathews from?

Q5 Who was Thomas Mathews's superior at the Battle of Cape Passaro?

Q6 Who was Thomas Mathews's second in command at the Battle of Toulon?

Q7 Why did Thomas Mathews leave the Royal Navy?

Q8 Thomas Mathews's grandfather, Thomas Armstrong, was executed for his involvement in what plot?

Q9 How many times did Thomas Mathews marry?

Q10 What was Thomas Mathews's flagship at the Battle of Toulon?

John Tovey

Q1 John Tovey was sometimes referred to by what other name?

Q2 What destroyer was John Tovey in command of at the Battle of Jutland?

Q3 John Tovey served as commander-in-chief of what fleet?

Q4 What position was John Tovey appointed to in 1943?

Q5 How many children did John Tovey have?

Q6 In what year did John Tovey retire from the Royal Navy?

Q7 What noble title did John Tovey receive?

Q8 What military award did John Tovey receive from the Soviet Union?

Q9 What school did John Tovey attend?

Q10 What country did John Tovey die in?

Walter Raleigh

Q1 How was Humphrey Gilbert related to Walter Raleigh?

Q2 Walter Raleigh was born in what English county?

Q3 What monarch ruled England when Walter Raleigh was executed?

Q4 Who did Walter Raleigh marry in secret?

Q5 What plot was Walter Raleigh involved in in 1603?

Q6 The Roanoke Colony was known by what other name?

Q7 In what year was Walter Raleigh knighted?

Q8 How was Walter Raleigh executed?

Q9 What product did Walter Raleigh help popularise in England?

Q10 What castle was Walter Raleigh imprisoned in on more than one occasion?

Andrew Cunningham

Q1 What noble title was Andrew Cunningham awarded?

Q2 What was Andrew Cunningham's nickname?

Q3 What city was Andrew Cunningham born in?

Q4 Andrew Cunningham was commander-in-chief of what fleet during the Second World War?

Q5 What position did Andrew Cunningham hold when he retired?

Q6 Where was Andrew Cunningham buried?

Q7 Andrew Cunningham was given command of what destroyer in 1911?

Q8 What was the first war that Andrew Cunningham served in?

Q9 What position did Andrew Cunningham hold at Elizabeth II's coronation?

Q10 In what war was Andrew Cunningham awarded the Distinguished Service Order?

Edward Vernon

Q1 What rank did Edward Vernon hold during the War of Jenkins' Ear?

Q2 Who did the Royal Navy fight at the Battle of Cartagena de Indias?

Q3 What was grog?

Q4 Edward Vernon was the namesake for what US President's estate?

Q5 Edward Vernon served as a Member of Parliament for what two constituencies?

Q6 What port in present-day Panama did Edward Vernon famously capture in 1739?

Q7 What political position did Edward Vernon's father, James Vernon, hold?

Q8 Where was Edward Vernon born?

Q9 In what year did Edward Vernon enter the Royal Navy?

Q10 What did Edward Vernon briefly rename Guantánamo Bay?

Cuthbert Collingwood

Q1 Whose commands did Cuthbert Collingwood succeed in 1805?

Q2 Where was Cuthbert Collingwood born?

Q3 What was the first Royal Navy ship that Cuthbert Collingwood sailed on?

Q4 Cuthbert Collingwood died on board what ship?

Q5 The HMS *Collingwood* is a stone frigate located in what town?

Q6 What was the last major battle that Cuthbert Collingwood took part in?

Q7 What noble title did Cuthbert Collingwood receive?

Q8 How old was Cuthbert Collingwood when he joined the Royal Navy?

Q9 What ship was Cuthbert Collingwood in charge of in 1781 when it was hit by a hurricane and wrecked?

Q10 What did Cuthbert Collingwood die from?

Edward Pellew

Q1 Where was Edward Pellew born?

Q2 Who was Edward Pellew's younger brother?

Q3 Edward Pellew served approximately how long in the Royal Navy?

Q4 What noble title did Edward Pellew receive?

Q5 Edward Pellew sailed to what archipelago during his maiden voyage?

Q6 Who named the Sir Edward Pellew Group of Islands?

Q7 Who did Edward Pellew marry?

Q8 What rank was Edward Pellew promoted to in 1804?

Q9 Before being pressed into the Royal Navy, what was Joseph Antonio Emidy's occupation?

Q10 What Royal Navy frigate was involved in the Action of 18 June 1793?

Charles Beresford

Q1 Charles Beresford was a member of what political party?

Q2 What Hawaiian did Charles Beresford propose to?

Q3 Charles Beresford was from what constituent country of the United Kingdom?

Q4 In what year did Charles Beresford receive a peerage?

Q5 Charles Beresford opposed reforms proposed by what Admiral of the Fleet?

Q6 In what year was Charles Beresford first elected as a Member of Parliament?

Q7 Charles Beresford received honours from how many foreign countries?

Q8 What rank was Charles Beresford promoted to in 1902?

Q9 What ship was Charles Beresford captain of between 1889 and 1893?

Q10 Between 1878 and 1881 Charles Beresford served as second in command of what royal yacht?

John Jellicoe

Q1 What fleet did John Jellicoe command at the Battle of Jutland?

Q2 John Jellicoe served as Governor-General of what country?

Q3 What did John Jellicoe become a member of in 1925?

Q4 Where was John Jellicoe buried?

Q5 In what year did John Jellicoe become First Sea Lord?

Q6 What ship did HMS *Victoria* collide with while John Jellicoe was on board?

Q7 John Jellicoe was trained on board what ship?

Q8 What shipping company did John Jellicoe's father work for?

Q9 Where was John Jellicoe born?

Q10 John Jellicoe supported the building of what new type of battleship in the first decade of the 20th century?

William Fitzwilliam Owen

Q1 What happened to William Fitzwilliam Owen at the age of four?

Q2 What rank was William Fitzwilliam Owen promoted to in 1841?

Q3 In what country did William Fitzwilliam Owen die?

Q4 What was the first ship William Fitzwilliam Owen sailed on as a member of the Royal Navy?

Q5 Where was William Fitzwilliam Owen held captive between 1808 and 1810?

Q6 Owen Sound is located in what Canadian province?

Q7 How was Edward Owen related to William Fitzwilliam Owen?

Q8 William Fitzwilliam Owen mapped part of the coast of what continent between 1821 and 1826?

Q9 A species of what animal were named in William Fitzwilliam Owen's honour by John Edward Gray?

Q10 William Fitzwilliam Owen was elected an Associate Fellow of what in 1844?

Alfred Chatfield

Q1 Alfred Chatfield served as commander-in-chief of what two fleets?

Q2 Alfred Chatfield was named as Minister for what in 1939?

Q3 Alfred Chatfield was born in what English county?

Q4 In what year did Alfred Chatfield join the Royal Navy?

Q5 What rank was Alfred Chatfield promoted to in 1904?

Q6 Alfred Chatfield served as whose Flag-Captain at the Battle of Heligoland Bight?

Q7 What peerage did Alfred Chatfield receive?

Q8 Alfred Chatfield served as a minister under what Prime Minister?

Q9 What ship was Alfred Chatfield on board at the Battle of Jutland?

Q10 Alfred Chatfield retired in what Buckinghamshire village?

Barrington Reynolds

Q1 How old was Barrington Reynolds when he was first captured by the French?

Q2 Barrington Reynolds was from what English county?

Q3 What rank did Barrington Reyonds's father have in the Royal Navy?

Q4 Barrington Reynolds played a key role in preventing what illegal trade?

Q5 What rank did Barrington Reynolds reach in 1811?

Q6 In what year did Barrington Reynolds become Commander-in-Chief, Plymouth?

Q7 How did Barrington Reynolds's father die?

Q8 What rank did Barrington Reynolds reach in the Royal Navy?

Q9 How old was Barrington Reynolds when he first went to sea?

Q10 In what village is Barrington Reynolds buried?

Edward Howard

Q1 In what century was Edward Howard born?

Q2 The Battle of Saint-Mathieu took place during what war?

Q3 Edward Howard's father was Duke of what?

Q4 What order of chivalry was Edward Howard awarded just prior to his death?

Q5 Edward Howard died while fighting against what country?

Q6 What was the Royal Navy's flagship at the Battle of Saint-Mathieu?

Q7 In what year did Edward Howard die?

Q8 Edward Howard served as what king's standard-bearer?

Q9 What Scottish sailor was in charge of the *Lion* when Edward Howard helped capture it?

Q10 When war broke out between England and France what rank was Edward Howard assigned?

Bertram Ramsay

Q1 What destroyer did Bertram Ramsay command during the First World War?

Q2 Bertram Ramsay was responsible for what evacuation?

Q3 How did Bertram Ramsay die?

Q4 Where was Bertram Ramsay born?

Q5 What rank was Bertram Ramsay promoted to in 1944?

Q6 How many children did Bertram Ramsay have?

Q7 What was the first Royal Navy ship Bertram Ramsay served on?

Q8 What Prime Minister persuaded Bertram Ramsay to come out of retirement?

Q9 In what year did Bertram Ramsay join the Royal Navy?

Q10 In what year did Bertram Ramsay receive the Order of the Bath?

John Leake

Q1 John Leake served as a Member of Parliament for what constituency?

Q2 In what London church is John Leake buried?

Q3 What position did John Leake hold between 1710 and 1712?

Q4 Who was John Leake's superior during the Battle of Málaga?

Q5 What ship was John Leake assigned to when he joined the Royal Navy?

Q6 What 1673 battle did John Leake take part in?

Q7 What rank was John Leake promoted to in 1689?

Q8 How many children did John Leake have with his wife?

Q9 John Leake donated a new altarpiece, communion-table, rails and pavement for the chancel of what church in 1710?

Q10 John Leake served as commander-in-chief of what colony?

Baldwin Wake Walker

Q1 What noble title did Baldwin Wake Walker receive?

Q2 What position did Baldwin Wake Walker hold between1848 and 1861?

Q3 What type of warships were introduced while Baldwin Wake Walker was in office?

Q4 What island was Baldwin Wake Walker born on?

Q5 What did Baldwin Wake Walker do in 1812?

Q6 What grandson of Baldwin Wake Walker played a leading role in the Dunkirk evacuation?

Q7 In what year was the steam-powered armoured frigate HMS *Warrior* launched?

Q8 How many times did Baldwin Wake Walker marry?

Q9 What expedition during the Greek War of Independence did Baldwin Wake Walker take part in?

Q10 Baldwin Wake Walker commanded what ship as flag captain in 1845?

John 'Jackie' Fisher

Q1 On how many occasions did John Fisher serve as First Sea Lord?

Q2 What colony was John Fisher born in?

Q3 What was the occupation of John Fisher's father?

Q4 How old was John Fisher when he joined the Royal Navy?

Q5 What was the first Royal Navy ship John Fisher sailed on?

Q6 What rank was John Fisher promoted to in 1869?

Q7 John Fisher is best known for doing what to the Royal Navy?

Q8 Who was John Fisher's wife?

Q9 John Fisher was chairman of what government board during the First World War?

Q10 Where was John Fisher's funeral held?

Robert Falcon Scott

Q1 What film was released in 1948 about Robert Falcon Scott?

Q2 On what ice shelf did Robert Falcon Scott die?

Q3 What two expeditions did Robert Falcon Scott lead to Antarctica?

Q4 Who else led an expedition to the South Pole shortly before Robert Falcon Scott's death?

Q5 Who was Robert Falcon Scott's wife?

Q6 How old was Robert Falcon Scott when he joined the Royal Navy?

Q7 What preparatory school did Robert Falcon Scott attend?

Q8 How old was Robert Falcon Scott when he died?

Q9 Robert Falcon Scott met Edward VII at what castle in 1904?

Q10 When Robert Falcon Scott's body was found, he was in possession of the first what ever discovered?

Charles Saunders

Q1 What ship did Charles Saunders command at the Second Battle of Cape Finisterre?

Q2 What position did Charles Saunders reach in the Mediterranean Fleet?

Q3 Charles Saunders served as commander-in-chief of what squadron between 1758 and 1759?

Q4 The Battle of the Plains of Abraham was fought near what city?

Q5 Where is Charles Saunders buried?

Q6 What two major wars did Charles Saunders take part in?

Q7 At what rank did Charles Saunders enter the Royal Navy?

Q8 Charles Saunders served as First Lord of the Admiralty under what Prime Minister?

Q9 Who named Cape Saunders in Charles Saunders's honour?

Q10 What order of chivalry did Charles Saunders receive in 1761?

Horace Hood

Q1 What rank did Horace Hood reach?

Q2 Horace Hood died during what battle?

Q3 In what year was the HMS *Invincible* sunk?

Q4 Horace Hood was awarded the Distinguished Service Order for his service on what continent?

Q5 How old was Horace Hood when he was installed as a Knight Commander of the Order of the Bath?

Q6 How was Horace Hood related to Samuel Hood?

Q7 In what place did Horace Hood graduate as a cadet in the Royal Navy?

Q8 What did Horace Hood do when he was 12?

Q9 What major war did Horace Hood serve in?

Q10 When Horace Hood became a captain in 1903, what ship was he put in command of?

John Cabot

Q1 John Cabot worked for what king?

Q2 What was John Cabot's name in his native language?

Q3 What present-day country was John Cabot from?

Q4 In what century was John Cabot born?

Q5 How was Sebastian Cabot related to John Cabot?

Q6 What continent did John Cabot famously travel to?

Q7 What was John Cabot's occupation?

Q8 What English port did John Cabot sail from on his first voyage?

Q9 Cabot Tower is located in what Canadian city?

Q10 Why is Cape Bonavista believed to be significant?

George Rooke

Q1 In what year did the Battle of Cádiz take place?

Q2 What rank did George Rooke reach in the Royal Navy?

Q3 George Rooke was born in what English county?

Q4 What king did George Rooke transport to England?

Q5 In what town is George Rooke buried?

Q6 How many times did George Rooke marry?

Q7 After being promoted to lieutenant, what ship was George Rooke assigned to?

Q8 In George Rooke's first battle, what country did he fight against?

Q9 What rank was George Rooke promoted to in 1690?

Q10 What two countries did George Rooke fight against at the Battle of Vigo Bay?

Robert FitzRoy

Q1 Robert FitzRoy is best known for being the captain of what ship?

Q2 Robert FitzRoy served as the Governor of what country?

Q3 Robert FitzRoy was born at what house?

Q4 How did Robert FitzRoy die?

Q5 What rank did Robert FitzRoy reach in the Royal Navy?

Q6 Robert FitzRoy was a fourth great-grandson of what king?

Q7 How was Robert FitzRoy related to Charles Augustus FitzRoy?

Q8 What college did Robert FitzRoy join at the age of 12?

Q9 Robert FitzRoy stood as what political party's candidate for Ipswich in the 1831 general election?

Q10 Robert FitzRoy was elected to what society in 1851?

John Jervis

Q1 John Jervis was Earl of what?

Q2 John Jervis served as a Member of Parliament for how many constituencies?

Q3 John Jervis is best remembered for what 1797 victory?

Q4 John Jervis was commander-in-chief of what fleet between 1795 and 1799?

Q5 What house was John Jervis born at?

Q6 What position did John Jervis hold in 1801?

Q7 What admiral agreed to give John Jervis a position in the Royal Navy?

Q8 How was John Jervis's wife related to him?

Q9 What did John Jervis do between 1772 and 1775?

Q10 In what year was John Jervis put in command of the Channel Fleet?

Augustus Keppel

Q1 What noble title was Augustus Keppel awarded?

Q2 Augustus Keppel served as a what between 1755 and 1782?

Q3 What rate of ship was the HMS *Maidstone*?

Q4 Augustus Keppel served as Commodore on what station?

Q5 Augustus Keppel served as commander-in-chief of what fleet?

Q6 Who was Augustus Keppel's second in command at the Battle of Ushant?

Q7 Augustus Keppel served as the First Lord of the Admiralty in the latter stages of what war?

Q8 What political party was Augustus Keppel a member of?

Q9 Who named Great Keppel Island in Augustus Keppel's honour?

Q10 What rank did Augustus Keppel reach in 1762?

William Gonson

Q1 What son of William Gonson would also pursue a career in the Royal Navy?

Q2 William Gonson served under what king?

Q3 What ship did William Gonson become the commander of in 1513?

Q4 To the nearest decade, how long did William Gonson serve as Clerk of Marine Causes?

Q5 William Gonson was appointed Vice Admiral of what two English counties in 1536?

Q6 Where was William Gonson born?

Q7 What position was William Gonson appointed to in 1524?

Q8 Before joining the Royal Navy, what was William Gonson's occupation?

Q9 How did William Gonson die?

Q10 What was the highest rank William Gonson reached in the Royal Navy?

Samuel Pepys

Q1 Samuel Pepys is most famous for writing what?

Q2 How old was Elisabeth Pepys when she married Samuel Pepys?

Q3 What university did Samuel Pepys attend?

Q4 In 1689 Samuel Pepys was imprisoned on suspicion of what?

Q5 Samuel Pepys served as Parliamentary and Financial Secretary to the Admiralty under what two monarchs?

Q6 What was Deb Willet's occupation?

Q7 The Pepys Library is located in what city?

Q8 What happened in London in 1666?

Q9 Samuel Pepys was born in a property on what London street?

Q10 How old was Samuel Pepys when he died?

Roger Keyes

Q1 Roger Keyes became a member of what in 1943?

Q2 Roger Keyes was a Member of Parliament for what constituency?

Q3 What present-day country was Roger Keyes born in?

Q4 What noble title was Roger Keyes awarded?

Q5 What was the occupation of Roger Keyes's father?

Q6 Roger Keyes was a member of what political party?

Q7 What country was Robert Keyes sent to in 1898?

Q8 Roger Keyes served as the liaison officer to what monarch?

Q9 Roger Keyes served as the first Director of what?

Q10 Roger Keyes helped to suppress what rebellion that took place between 1899 and 1901?

George Byng

Q1 George Byng was Viscount what?

Q2 George Byng served as First Lord of the Admiralty during the reign of what monarch?

Q3 George Byng resided on an estate in what Bedfordshire village?

Q4 Who did George Byng serve under at the Capture of Gibraltar?

Q5 In what year did the Battle of Cape Passaro take place?

Q6 George Byng joined the Royal Navy in what capacity?

Q7 What was the first Royal Navy ship George Byng served on?

Q8 George Byng's marriage took place at what church?

Q9 What academy was established in 1833?

Q10 George Byng became flag captain of what ship in 1693?

Adam Duncan

Q1 Who did the Royal Navy fight at the Battle of Camperdown?

Q2 In what year was the Battle of Camperdown fought?

Q3 What noble title was Adam Duncan awarded?

Q4 What country was Adam Duncan from?

Q5 What rank did Adam Duncan reach in the Royal Navy?

Q6 What was the first Royal Navy ship Adam Duncan served on?

Q7 What medal was Adam Duncan awarded?

Q8 Andrew Duncan took part in what war that was fought between 1756 and 1763?

Q9 In what year did Adam Duncan join the Royal Navy?

Q10 What position was Adam Duncan appointed to in 1795?

George Anson

Q1 What French admiral did George Anson defeat at the First Battle of Cape Finisterre?

Q2 In what year was the First Battle of Cape Finisterre fought?

Q3 George Anson became First Lord of the Admiralty during what war?

Q4 George Anson served as First Lord of the Admiralty under how many Prime Ministers?

Q5 What English county was George Anson born in?

Q6 George Anson joined the Royal Navy during what war?

Q7 At what mansion did George Anson die?

Q8 George Anson became a Member of what in 1744?

Q9 In what year did George Anson become Lord Anson?

Q10 George Anson circumnavigated the globe during what war?

Edward Berry

Q1 What noble title was Edward Berry awarded?

Q2 Edward Berry was flag captain of what ship during the Battle of the Nile?

Q3 Edward Berry was commander of what ship during the Battle of Trafalgar?

Q4 Edward Berry died in what city?

Q5 In what year did the Battle of San Domingo take place?

Q6 What order of chivalry was Edward Berry awarded in 1815?

Q7 How old was Edward Berry when he joined the Royal Navy?

Q8 What relation took charge of Edward Berry's education?

Q9 What rank was Edward Berry promoted to in 1794?

Q10 Edward Berry caught Horatio Nelson when he was injured during what battle?

Samuel Hood

Q1 Samuel Hood served as commander-in-chief of what fleet?

Q2 The Battle of the Mona Passage was fought during what war?

Q3 What was Samuel Hood's father's occupation?

Q4 What did Samuel Hood do in 1741?

Q5 Samuel Hood became commander of what sloop in 1754?

Q6 Who was Samuel Hood's superior at the Battle of the Saintes?

Q7 What island did Samuel Hood successfully invade in 1794?

Q8 How old was Samuel Hood when he died?

Q9 What country did Samuel Hood fight at the Battle of the Mona Passage?

Q10 Samuel Hood served as Governor of what hospital?

William Cornwallis

Q1 What was William Cornwallis's nickname?

Q2 How was William Cornwallis related to Charles Cornwallis?

Q3 How old was William Cornwallis when he took part in the Siege of Louisbourg?

Q4 What rank did William Cornwallis reach in the Royal Navy?

Q5 William Cornwallis served as a Member of Parliament for what two constituencies?

Q6 What was the first Royal Navy ship William Cornwallis served on?

Q7 How many times did William Cornwallis marry?

Q8 Cornwallis's Retreat took place during what war?

Q9 What yacht did William Cornwallis command in 1783?

Q10 In what year did William Cornwallis incur a court martial?

James Saumarez

Q1 On what date was the Second Battle of Algeciras fought?

Q2 Where was the Second Battle of Algeciras fought?

Q3 What two countries was the Second Battle of Algeciras fought against?

Q4 What island was James Saumarez born on?

Q5 What rank did James Saumarez reach in the Royal Navy?

Q6 What ship did James Saumarez command at the Battle of the Saintes?

Q7 The Action of 20 October 1793 took place during what war?

Q8 Who was James Saumarez's superior at the Battle of the Nile?

Q9 What position did James Saumarez hold between 1824 and 1827?

Q10 What fleet was James Saumarez given command of in 1808?

Thomas Cochrane

Q1 Who nicknamed Thomas Cochrane *Le Loup des Mers* 'The Sea Wolf'?

Q2 What happened to Thomas Cochrane in 1814?

Q3 Thomas Cochrane served in how many country's navies?

Q4 In what year was the Liberating Expedition of Peru organised?

Q5 Jack Aubrey was a fictional character created by what writer?

Q6 What country was Thomas Cochrane born in?

Q7 What was Thomas Cochrane granted in 1832?

Q8 Thomas Cochrane was Earl of what?

Q9 How many times did Thomas Cochrane marry?

Q10 In what year did Thomas Cochrane first become a Member of Parliament?

Maurice Suckling

Q1 How was Maurice Suckling related to Horatio Nelson?

Q2 What rank did Maurice Suckling reach in the Royal Navy?

Q3 What did Maurice Suckling become in 1775?

Q4 How was Catherine Suckling related to Maurice Suckling?

Q5 What English county was Maurice Suckling from?

Q6 What was Maurice Suckling's first position in the Royal Navy?

Q7 What was the first Royal Navy ship Maurice Suckling served on?

Q8 Maurice Suckling was the commander of what ship at the Battle of Cap-Français?

Q9 Who did Maurice Suckling succeed as the Member of Parliament for Portsmouth?

Q10 How old was Maurice Suckling when he left home to join the Royal Navy?

Frederick Marryat

Q1 Frederick Marryat was a friend of what famous novelist?

Q2 Frederick Marryat is best known for writing what 1836 novel?

Q3 What children's novel did Frederick Marryat have published in 1847?

Q4 Marryat's Code was a system of what?

Q5 Who was Frederick Marryat's father?

Q6 At what rank did Frederick Marryat join the Royal Navy?

Q7 What was the first Royal Navy ship Frederick Marryat served on?

Q8 What magazine did Frederick Marryat edit between 1832 and 1835?

Q9 Why did Frederick Marryat leave the Royal Navy?

Q10 What war did Frederick Marryat fight in against the USA?

David Beatty

Q1 What noble title did David Beatty hold?

Q2 What squadron did David Beatty command at the Battle of Jutland?

Q3 Who did David Beatty succeed as Commander-in-Chief of the Grand Fleet?

Q4 David Beatty was involved in negotiating what 1922 treaty?

Q5 What English county was David Beatty born in?

Q6 David Beatty received his training as a Royal Navy cadet in what town?

Q7 David Beatty's first commission in the Royal Navy was on board whose flagship?

Q8 What position was David Beatty appointed to in 1919?

Q9 On what continent was the Mahdist War fought?

Q10 In what year did David Beatty retire from the Royal Navy?

Dudley Pound

Q1 What island was Dudley Pound born on?

Q2 Dudley Pound participated in what famous 1916 battle?

Q3 In what year were the HMS *Prince of Wales* and HMS *Repulse* sunk?

Q4 What position was Dudley Pound appointed to in 1939?

Q5 Dudley Pound died during what war?

Q6 What country was Dudley Pound's mother from?

Q7 What was the occupation of Dudley Pound's father?

Q8 What training ship did Dudley Pound join as a cadet in 1891?

Q9 Dudley Pound became commander of what battlecruiser in 1919?

Q10 What did Dudley Pound die from?

Christopher Cradock

Q1 Christopher Cradock was killed during what battle?

Q2 What rank did Christopher Cradock reach in the Royal Navy?

Q3 What was Christopher Cradock's flagship when he died?

Q4 What yacht was Christopher Cradock appointed to in 1894?

Q5 What was the name of Christopher Cradock's first book?

Q6 What Prussian order of chivalry did Christopher Cradock receive?

Q7 What animal accompanied Christopher Cradock at sea?

Q8 What English county was Christopher Cradock from?

Q9 At the start of the First World War, Christopher Cradock was charged with finding and destroying what squadron of the Imperial German Navy?

Q10 The Battle of the Taku Forts was fought during what rebellion?

Somerset Gough-Calthorpe

Q1 Somerset Gough-Calthorpe served as a junior officer in what African war?

Q2 Somerset Gough-Calthorpe died on what island?

Q3 Somerset Gough-Calthorpe became Second Sea Lord during what war?

Q4 In what year was the Armistice of Mudros signed?

Q5 Somerset Gough-Calthorpe became commander-in-chief of what fleet in 1917?

Q6 The Occupation of Constantinople lasted for approximately how many years?

Q7 What class of battleship was the HMS *Superb* (1907)?

Q8 In what year did Somerset Gough-Calthorpe retire from the Royal Navy?

Q9 What industrialist and politician was Somerset Gough-Calthorpe's father-in-law?

Q10 What position was Somerset Gough-Calthorpe appointed to in 1920?

Louis Mountbatten

Q1 Louis Mountbatten was Earl of what?

Q2 Who was Louis Mountbatten's father?

Q3 What title did Louis Mountbatten hold between 1947 and 1948?

Q4 In what year did Louis Mountbatten become First Sea Lord?

Q5 Louis Mountbatten became a Member of what in 1947?

Q6 Louis Mountbatten was born in what house?

Q7 What university did Louis Mountbatten attend?

Q8 Who was Louis Mountbatten's wife?

Q9 Louis Mountbatten was assassinated by what terrorist group?

Q10 Louis Mountbatten served as Chairman of what between 1960 and 1961?

Tom Phillips

Q1 What was Tom Phillips's nickname?

Q2 What squadron did Tom Phillips command during the Japanese invasion of Malaya?

Q3 What ship did Tom Phillips die on board?

Q4 Tom Phillips died during what war?

Q5 What rank did Tom Phillips reach in the Royal Navy?

Q6 Tom Phillips was born in what English county?

Q7 What school did Tom Phillips attend?

Q8 Tom Phillips assumed command of what destroyer in 1928?

Q9 What Royal Navy training establishment did Tom Phillips attend between 1919 and 1920?

Q10 What was most notable about Tom Phillips's physical appearance?

William Parker

Q1 How old was William Parker when he took part in the Glorious First of June?

Q2 What was the first war William Parker took part in?

Q3 Who was William Parker's father?

Q4 William Parker was from what English county?

Q5 How many French ships were captured during the Action of 13 March 1806?

Q6 What position did William Parker hold between 1841 and 1844?

Q7 A monument was erected in William Parker's memory at what cathedral?

Q8 William Parker served as First Sea Lord under what Prime Minister?

Q9 What did William Parker do in 1857?

Q10 What noble title was William Parker awarded?

Francis Harvey

Q1 Francis Harvey was awarded the Victoria Cross for his actions during what battle?

Q2 Francis Harvey died on board what ship?

Q3 What rank did Francis Harvey reach in the Royal Navy?

Q4 Francis Harvey was born in what English county?

Q5 How was Captain John Harvey related to Francis Harvey?

Q6 What war did Francis Harvey fight in?

Q7 Where was Francis Harvey buried?

Q8 Francis Harvey was a member of what arm of the Royal Navy?

Q9 What rank did Francis Harvey's great-grandad, Edward Harvey, reach in the Royal Navy?

Q10 In what year did Francis Harvey join the Royal Navy?

Cloudesley Shovell

Q1 Cloudesley Shovell died during what disaster?

Q2 The Battles of Barfleur and La Hougue took place during what war?

Q3 Cloudesley Shovell served as a Member of Parliament for what constituency?

Q4 Cloudesley Shovell's first name derives from the surname of what relative?

Q5 In what role did Cloudesley Shovell enter the Royal Navy?

Q6 In what year was the Battle of Bantry Bay fought?

Q7 Who was Cloudesley Shovell's superior at the Capture of Gibraltar?

Q8 What rank did Cloudesley Shovell reach in the Royal Navy?

Q9 Cloudesley Shovell's wife had previously been married to what naval commander?

Q10 Where is Cloudesley Shovell buried?

James Somerville

Q1 What country's fleet did the Royal Navy target during the Attack on Mers-el-Kébir?

Q2 What force did James Somerville command during the Second World War?

Q3 What rank did James Somerville hold while serving on board the HMS *Royal Arthur*?

Q4 What rank did James Somerville reach in the Royal Navy?

Q5 What was James Somerville's role at the start of the First World War?

Q6 James Somerville died at what house?

Q7 What position was James Somerville appointed to in 1942?

Q8 After his retirement from the Royal Navy, James Somerville served as what?

Q9 How is the newsreader Julia Somerville related to James Somerville?

Q10 What order of chivalry was James Somerville awarded in 1941?

Richard Howe

Q1 In what year did the Glorious First of June take place?

Q2 Richard Howe's father served as Governor of what?

Q3 What ship did Richard Howe serve on board at the Battle of Quiberon Bay?

Q4 The Great Siege of Gibraltar took place during what war?

Q5 What noble title did Richard Howe receive?

Q6 Richard Howe was born in what city?

Q7 Richard Howe helped to resolve what 1797 mutiny?

Q8 In what year did Richard Howe become a full admiral?

Q9 How was Richard Howe related to General William Howe?

Q10 Richard Howe served as First Lord of the Admiralty under what two Prime Ministers?

Robert Blake

Q1 Where was Robert Blake originally buried?

Q2 What side did Robert Blake support in the English Civil War?

Q3 Robert Blake's nephew, Joseph Blake, served as Governor of what?

Q4 What nickname is sometimes given to Robert Blake?

Q5 Robert Blake was elected a Member of Parliament for what constituency in 1640?

Q6 What army did Robert Blake fight in?

Q7 Robert Blake was promoted to lieutenant colonel after what siege?

Q8 In what year was Robert Blake appointed general at sea?

Q9 What was issued featuring Robert Blake in 1982?

Q10 What did Robert Blake serve as between 1656 and 1657?

Battles

Battle of Trafalgar

Q1 The Battle of Trafalgar was fought between the Royal Navy and the navies of what two other countries?

Q2 In what year did the Battle of Trafalgar take place?

Q3 What was the Royal Navy's flagship at the Battle of Trafalgar?

Q4 What admiral is believed to have been murdered shortly after the Battle of Trafalgar?

Q5 Who was Prime Minister at the time of the Battle of Trafalgar?

Q6 Who painted *The Battle of Trafalgar, as Seen from the Mizen Starboard Shrouds of the Victory* in 1806?

Q7 The Battle of Trafalgar was fought during what war?

Q8 What country was Federico Gravina from?

Q9 Who was Horatio Nelson's second in command at the Battle of Trafalgar?

Q10 How many ships of the line did the Royal Navy have at the Battle of Trafalgar?

Battle of Beachy Head

Q1 In what year was the Battle of Beachy Head fought?

Q2 The Battle of Beachy Head was fought during what war?

Q3 What country was victorious at the Battle of Beachy Head?

Q4 In what body of water was the Battle of Beachy Head fought?

Q5 How many days did the Battle of Beachy Head last?

Q6 Who were the English allied with at the Battle of Beachy Head?

Q7 Who ruled England at the time of the Battle of Beachy Head?

Q8 Who led English forces at the Battle of Beachy Head?

Q9 How many ships did the Royal Navy's opponents lose during the Battle of Beachy Head?

Q10 Who led the Royal Navy's opponents at the Battle of Beachy Head?

Battle of Dogger Bank

Q1 The Battle of Dogger Bank was fought in what sea?

Q2 What Royal Navy fleet took part in the Battle of Dogger Bank?

Q3 What side won the Battle of Dogger Bank?

Q4 The Battle of Dogger Bank was fought during what war?

Q5 In what year was the Battle of Dogger Bank fought?

Q6 Who led the Royal Navy at the Battle of Dogger Bank?

Q7 What country's navy did the Royal Navy fight at the Battle of Dogger Bank?

Q8 Who led the Royal Navy's opponents at the Battle of Dogger Bank?

Q9 What ship served as flagship of the 1st Battlecruiser Squadron?

Q10 What ship was sunk at the Battle of Dogger Bank?

Battle of Cape St Vincent

Q1 The Battle of Cape St Vincent was fought in what part of the Napoleonic Wars?

Q2 Who commanded the Royal Navy at the Battle of Cape St Vincent?

Q3 The Battle of Cape St Vincent was fought off the coast of what country?

Q4 Who was the Spanish commander at the Battle of Cape St Vincent?

Q5 In what year did the Battle of Cape St Vincent take place?

Q6 Who won the Battle of Cape St Vincent?

Q7 What was the Royal Navy's flagship at the Battle of Cape St Vincent?

Q8 What was the largest ship afloat at the time of the Battle of Cape St Vincent?

Q9 How many guns did Spain's flagship have at the Battle of Cape St Vincent?

Q10 Who received the surrender of the *San Nicholas*?

First Battle of Cape Finisterre

Q1 Who commanded the Royal Navy at the First Battle of Cape Finisterre?

Q2 The First Battle of Cape Finisterre was fought during what war?

Q3 In what ocean was the First Battle of Cape Finisterre fought?

Q4 How many ships of the line did the Royal Navy have at the First Battle of Cape Finisterre?

Q5 Who commanded the Royal Navy's opponent during the First Battle of Finisterre?

Q6 What country did the Royal Navy fight against at the First Battle of Cape Finisterre?

Q7 In what year was the First Battle of Cape Finisterre fought?

Q8 What was the Royal Navy's flagship at the First Battle of Cape Finisterre?

Q9 How many months after the First Battle of Cape Finisterre did the Second Battle of Cape Finisterre take place?

Q10 The First Battle of Cape Finisterre involved the Royal Navy attacking what?

The Glorious First of June

Q1 In what ocean was the Glorious First of June fought?

Q2 In what year was the Glorious First of June fought?

Q3 Who commanded the Royal Navy during the Glorious First of June?

Q4 Who commanded the French Navy during the Glorious First of June?

Q5 What French ship of the line was sunk during the Glorious First of June?

Q6 Who was King of Great Britain at the time of the Glorious First of June?

Q7 What Royal Navy fleet took part in the Glorious First of June?

Q8 What was the French convoy carrying during the Glorious First of June?

Q9 The Glorious First of June was part of what Royal Navy campaign?

Q10 What was the Royal Navy's flagship during the Glorious First of June?

Battle of Jutland

Q1 In what sea was the Battle of Jutland fought?

Q2 Who commanded the Royal Navy at the Battle of Jutland?

Q3 In what year did the Battle of Jutland take place?

Q4 What German fleet took part in the Battle of Jutland?

Q5 The Battle of Jutland was fought over how many days?

Q6 Who commanded the Imperial German Navy at the Battle of Jutland?

Q7 Who won the Battle of Jutland?

Q8 What Royal Navy fleet took part in the Battle of Jutland?

Q9 Germany sought to destroy the Royal Navy's principal fleet at the Battle of Jutland in order to do what?

Q10 The Battle of Jutland took place during what war?

D-Day

Q1 The D-Day landings took place in what region of France?

Q2 What was D-Day's codename?

Q3 In what year did D-Day take place?

Q4 What operation intended to mislead the German high command regarding the time and place of the D-Day landings?

Q5 What extensive system of coastal defences did Germany build in continental Europe?

Q6 What nicknames were given to the five main landing areas?

Q7 D-Day laid the foundations for Allied victory in what theatre of the Second World War?

Q8 Other than the United Kingdom, what country was the main contributor to the D-Day landings?

Q9 The Allied forces were divided into how many armies during D-Day?

Q10 D-Day began with the liberation of what country?

Battle of the Atlantic

Q1 In what years did the Battle of the Atlantic take place?

Q2 The Battle of the Atlantic was the longest continual military campaign of what war?

Q3 What two countries did the Royal Navy fight against in the Battle of the Atlantic?

Q4 In what year was the *Bismarck* sunk?

Q5 When did the USA join the Battle of the Atlantic?

Q6 How many people held the post of Commander-in-Chief, Western Approaches during the Battle of the Atlantic?

Q7 The Royal Navy imposed what on its opponents at the start of the Battle of the Atlantic?

Q8 What was the *Kriegsmarine*?

Q9 In what battle was HMS *Hood* sunk?

Q10 In what year did the Channel Dash take place?

Battle of Scheveningen

Q1 The Battle of Scheveningen was fought during what war?

Q2 What was the official name of England at the time of the Battle of Scheveningen?

Q3 What commander was killed during the Battle of Scheveningen?

Q4 What country did the Royal Navy fight during the Battle of Scheveningen?

Q5 How many ships did the Royal Navy have at the Battle of Scheveningen?

Q6 In what year did the Battle of Scheveningen take place?

Q7 The Battle of Scheveningen was fought off the coast of what present-day country?

Q8 Who won the Battle of Scheveningen?

Q9 Who led the Royal Navy during the Battle of Scheveningen?

Q10 A sniper from whose ship killed the commander of the Royal Navy's opponent during the Battle of Scheveningen?

Battle of Lowestoft

Q1 The Battle of Lowestoft was fought off the coast of what English county?

Q2 The Battle of Lowestoft was fought during what war?

Q3 What future king commanded the Royal Navy at the Battle of Lowestoft?

Q4 What commander of the Royal Navy's opponent was killed during the Battle of Lowestoft?

Q5 What country's navy did the Royal Navy fight at the Battle of Lowestoft?

Q6 How many guns did the HMS *Royal Charles* have?

Q7 What side won the Battle of Lowestoft?

Q8 In what year did the Battle of Lowestoft take place?

Q9 How many squadrons was the Royal Navy's fleet composed of during the Battle of Lowestoft?

Q10 What was the flagship of the Royal Navy's opponent at the Battle of Lowestoft?

Battle of Sluys

Q1 In what year was the Battle of Sluys fought?

Q2 Who was King of England at the time of the Battle of Sluys?

Q3 The Battle of Sluys was fought during what war?

Q4 What two commanders of the Royal Navy's opponent were killed during the Battle of Sluys?

Q5 What country did the Royal Navy fight during the Battle of Sluys?

Q6 The Battle of Sluys was known by what other name?

Q7 The Battle of Sluys was fought off the coast of what present-day country?

Q8 What Lord High Admiral served at the Battle of Sluys?

Q9 What river did the Royal Navy sail from prior to the Battle of Sluys?

Q10 The Battle of Sluys was commemorated on what kind of coin?

Raid on the Medway

Q1 The Raid on the Medway occurred during what war?

Q2 What Prince led the Royal Navy during the Raid on the Medway?

Q3 What side won the Raid on the Medway?

Q4 What flagship was captured during the Raid on the Medway?

Q5 In what year did the Raid on the Medway take place?

Q6 The Raid on the Medway occurred near what dockyard?

Q7 How many days did the Raid on the Medway last?

Q8 What castle was supposed to provide protection for English ships?

Q9 Who were the two main commanders of the Royal Navy's opponent at the Raid on the Medway?

Q10 What was the occupation of Pieter Cornelisz van Soest?

Battle of San Carlos

Q1 The Battle of San Carlos was fought during what war?

Q2 In what year was the Battle of San Carlos fought?

Q3 How long did the Battle of San Carlos last?

Q4 Who won the Battle of San Carlos?

Q5 Who commanded the Royal Navy at the Battle of San Carlos?

Q6 What destroyer was sunk during the Battle of San Carlos?

Q7 What country did the Royal Navy fight against during the Battle of San Carlos?

Q8 How many Royal Navy ships were sunk during the Battle of San Carlos?

Q9 What position did Mario Menéndez hold during the Battle of San Carlos?

Q10 Who was Prime Minister at the time of the Battle of San Carlos?

Battle of the Nile

Q1 The Battle of the Nile is known by what other name?

Q2 In what year did the Battle of the Nile take place?

Q3 The Battle of the Nile lasted for how many days?

Q4 What French commander died during the Battle of the Nile?

Q5 Who led the Royal Navy at the Battle of the Nile?

Q6 What was the French flagship at the Battle of the Nile?

Q7 The Battle of the Nile was fought in what empire?

Q8 What does the term 'band of brothers' refer to?

Q9 Who wrote the poem *Casabianca*?

Q10 How many ships of the line did both navies have at the Battle of the Nile?

Dunkirk evacuation

Q1 How many days did the Dunkirk evacuation last?

Q2 In what year did the Dunkirk evacuation take place?

Q3 The Dunkirk evacuation took place in what country?

Q4 What was the Dunkirk evacuation's codename?

Q5 To the nearest 100,000, how many soldiers were evacuated in the Dunkirk evacuation?

Q6 The Dunkirk evacuation was part of what battle?

Q7 What famous speech by Winston Churchill followed the Dunkirk evacuation?

Q8 Who led German forces during the Dunkirk evacuation?

Q9 Who was responsible for the Dunkirk evacuation?

Q10 In order for the Dunkirk evacuation to be a success, the Royal Navy relied on a large number of what?

Battle of the Chesapeake

Q1 In what war was the Battle of the Chesapeake fought?

Q2 The Battle of the Chesapeake was known by what other name?

Q3 Who led the Royal Navy at the Battle of the Chesapeake?

Q4 In what ocean was the Battle of the Chesapeake fought?

Q5 Who led the French Navy at the Battle of the Chesapeake?

Q6 What side won the Battle of the Chesapeake?

Q7 What was the French flagship at the Battle of the Chesapeake?

Q8 What was the Royal Navy's flagship during the Battle of the Chesapeake?

Q9 What Royal Navy ship was scuttled during the Battle of the Chesapeake?

Q10 Where did the Royal Navy's fleet sail to after the Battle of the Chesapeake?

Battle of Quiberon Bay

Q1 The Battle of Quiberon Bay was fought off the coast of what country?

Q2 What side won the Battle of Quiberon Bay?

Q3 The Battle of Quiberon Bay was fought during what war?

Q4 Who led the Royal Navy at the Battle of Quiberon Bay?

Q5 What was France's flagship during the Battle of Quiberon Bay?

Q6 What was the Royal Navy's flagship at the Battle of Quiberon Bay?

Q7 Who led the French at the Battle of Quiberon Bay?

Q8 In what year did the Battle of Quiberon Bay take place?

Q9 In what year was the HMAS *Quiberon* launched?

Q10 How many ships of the line did the Royal Navy have at the Battle of Quiberon Bay?

Battle of the Saintes

Q1 The Battle of the Saintes took place during what war?

Q2 How many days did the Battle of the Saintes last?

Q3 Who led the Royal Navy during the Battle of the Saintes?

Q4 What side won the Battle of the Saintes?

Q5 Before the Battle of the Saintes France and Spain had been planning on invading what island?

Q6 What pioneering tactic was used during the Battle of the Saintes?

Q7 The Battle of the Saintes is named after a group of islands in what region of the Atlantic Ocean?

Q8 In what year did the Battle of the Saintes take place?

Q9 Who led the French Navy during the Battle of the Saintes?

Q10 What was the Royal Navy's flagship at the Battle of the Saintes?

First Battle of Heligoland Bight

Q1 The First Battle of Heligoland Bight was the first naval battle of what war?

Q2 The First Battle of Heligoland Bight was fought in what sea?

Q3 What German commander was killed during the First Battle of Heligoland Bight?

Q4 Who won the First Battle of Heligoland Bight?

Q5 Who led the Royal Navy during the First Battle of Heligoland Bight?

Q6 In what year did the First Battle of Heligoland Bight take place?

Q7 How many days did the First Battle of Heligoland Bight last for?

Q8 How many Royal Navy ships were sunk during the First Battle of Heligoland Bight?

Q9 How many German destroyers were sunk during the First Battle of Heligoland Bight?

Q10 Who led the Imperial German Navy during the First Battle of Heligoland Bight?

Battle of Camperdown

Q1 Who led the Royal Navy at the Battle of Camperdown?

Q2 The Battle of Camperdown was fought during what war?

Q3 What Royal Navy fleet took part in the Battle of Camperdown?

Q4 The Battle of Camperdown was fought between the Royal Navy and what present-day county?

Q5 Who was the commander of the Royal Navy's opponent during the Battle of Camperdown?

Q6 What was the Royal Navy's flagship during the Battle of Camperdown?

Q7 In what year did the Battle of Camperdown take place?

Q8 What was the flagship of the Royal Navy's opponent during the Battle of Camperdown?

Q9 What mutinies occurred in the Royal Navy in the same year as the Battle of Camperdown?

Q10 Who was Prime Minister at the time of the Battle of Camperdown?

Battle of the Falkland Islands

Q1 The Battle of the Falkland Islands took place during what war?

Q2 In what ocean did the Battle of the Falkland Islands take place?

Q3 What squadron was destroyed during the Battle of the Falkland Islands?

Q4 Who led the Royal Navy at the Battle of the Falkland Islands?

Q5 What German commander died during the Battle of the Falkland Islands?

Q6 In what year did the Battle of the Falkland Islands take place?

Q7 Where is the Battle of the Falkland Islands celebrated as a public holiday?

Q8 What type of ship was the HMS *Invincible*?

Q9 Out of 8 vessels, how many German ships survived the Battle of the Falkland Islands?

Q10 How many days did the Battle of the Falkland Islands last?

The Four Days' Battle

Q1 The Four Days' Battle was fought during what war?

Q2 The Four Days' Battle was fought off the coast of what country?

Q3 What two key English commanders were killed during the Four Days' Battle?

Q4 What two key Dutch commanders were killed during the Four Days' War?

Q5 In what year did the Four Days' War take place?

Q6 Who was King of England when the Four Days' War took place?

Q7 What is the Four Days' Battle best known for?

Q8 What side won the Four Days' Battle?

Q9 What was the Royal Navy's flagship during the Four Days' Battle?

Q10 How many days did the Four Days' Battle last?

First Battle of Algeciras

Q1 Who led the Royal Navy during the First Battle of Algeciras?

Q2 What two countries did the Royal Navy fight against during the First Battle of Algeciras?

Q3 The First Battle of Algeciras was fought during what war?

Q4 In what year was the First Battle of Algeciras fought?

Q5 The First Battle of Algeciras was fought off the coast of what peninsular?

Q6 How many days after the First Battle of Algeciras did the Second Battle of Algeciras take place?

Q7 What Royal Navy ship was captured during the First Battle of Algeciras?

Q8 Who commanded the Royal Navy's opponent during the First Battle of Algeciras?

Q9 Solomon Ferris was captain of what ship during the First Battle of Algeciras?

Q10 The Royal Navy had six ships of the line at the First Battle of Algeciras. How many did its opponents have?

Spanish Armada

Q1 Who ruled England at the time of the Spanish Armada?

Q2 Who was King of Spain at the time of the Spanish Armada?

Q3 In what year did the Spanish Armada sail for England?

Q4 Who commanded the Royal Navy against the Spanish Armada?

Q5 What Tavistock-born privateer played a key role in defeating the Spanish Armada?

Q6 The Spanish Armada was part of what war?

Q7 The English monarch famously gave a speech in what Essex village at the time of the Spanish Armada?

Q8 The Spanish Armada was triggered partly as a result of English intervention in what Spanish territory?

Q9 Who commanded the Spanish Armada?

Q10 The Royal Navy sailed from what port to attack the Spanish Armada?

Second Battle of Cape Finisterre

Q1 The Second Battle of Cape Finisterre was fought during what war?

Q2 Who led the Royal Navy at the Second Battle of Cape Finisterre?

Q3 Who commanded the French Navy at the Second Battle of Cape Finisterre?

Q4 The Second Battle of Finisterre was fought off the coast of what country?

Q5 In what year was the Second Battle of Cape Finisterre fought?

Q6 How many ships of the line did the Royal Navy capture at the Second Battle of Cape Finisterre?

Q7 How many ships of the line did the Royal Navy have at the Second Battle of Cape Finisterre?

Q8 How many ships were sunk at the Second Battle of Cape Finisterre?

Q9 Who commanded the HMS *Devonshire* at the Second Battle of Cape Finisterre?

Q10 What was the French flagship at the Second Battle of Cape Finisterre?

Battles of Barfleur and La Hougue

Q1 In what year did the Battles of Barfleur and La Hougue take place?

Q2 The Battles of Barfleur and La Hougue took place during what war?

Q3 The Battles of Barfleur and La Hougue were fought off the coast of what country?

Q4 What country was England allied with at the Battles of Barfleur and La Hougue?

Q5 Who led the Royal Navy at the Battles of Barfleur and La Hougue?

Q6 Who was in charge of the French Navy at the Battles of Barfleur and La Hougue?

Q7 Who won the Battles of Barfleur and La Hougue?

Q8 How many ships of the line did France have at the Battles of Barfleur and La Hougue?

Q9 Who ruled England at the time of the Battles of Barfleur and La Hougue?

Q10 The Battles of Barfleur and La Hougue ended the threat of what?

Siege of Lyme Regis

Q1 The Siege of Lyme Regis was fought during what war?

Q2 What two sides fought each other at the Siege of Lyme Regis?

Q3 In what year did the Siege of Lyme Regis take place?

Q4 The Siege of Lyme Regis lasted for how many weeks?

Q5 The Siege of Lyme Regis took place in what English county?

Q6 Lyme Regis was important because it controlled the shipping route between the English Channel and what city?

Q7 Who led the siege on Lyme Regis?

Q8 Who was King of England at the time of the Siege of Lyme Regis?

Q9 What side did Robert Blake support at the Siege of Lyme Regis?

Q10 The Siege of Lyme Regis ended when who sent a relief force?

Battle of Portland

Q1 The Battle of Portland is known by what other name?

Q2 The Battle of Portland was fought during what war?

Q3 What was the official name of England at the time of the Battle of Portland?

Q4 The Battle of Portland was fought in what body of water?

Q5 Who commanded the forces of the Royal Navy's opposition at the Battle of Portland?

Q6 In what year was the Battle of Portland fought?

Q7 Who commanded the Royal Navy at the Battle of Portland?

Q8 What side won the Battle of Portland?

Q9 What was the flagship of the Royal Navy's opponent at the Battle of Portland?

Q10 The Battle of Portland lasted for how many days?

Attack on Mers-el-Kébir

Q1 The Attack on Mers-el-Kébir was part of what naval campaign?

Q2 In what year did the Attack on Mers-el-Kébir take place?

Q3 The Attack on Mers-el-Kébir was a Royal Navy assault against what country's navy?

Q4 The Attack on Mers-el-Kébir occurred off the coast of what continent?

Q5 What battleship was sunk during the Attack on Mers-el-Kébir?

Q6 What was the Royal Navy's flagship at the Attack on Mers-el-Kébir?

Q7 What was the flagship of the Royal Navy's opponent at the Attack on Mers-el-Kébir?

Q8 What side won the Attack on Mers-el-Kébir?

Q9 Who was in charge of the Royal Navy at the Attack on Mers-el-Kébir?

Q10 Who commanded the forces of the Royal Navy's opponent at the Attack on Mers-el-Kébir?

Battle of Winchelsea

Q1 In what year did the Battle of Winchelsea take place?

Q2 Who was King of England at the time of the Battle of Winchelsea?

Q3 Who did the Royal Navy fight against at the Battle of Winchelsea?

Q4 Who commanded the forces of the Royal Navy's opponent at the Battle of Winchelsea?

Q5 What side won the Battle of Winchelsea?

Q6 The Battle of Winchelsea was part of what war?

Q7 The Battle of Winchelsea was fought in what body of water?

Q8 What does the alternative name for the Battle of Winchelsea, the 'Battle of Les Espagnols sur Mer', mean in English?

Q9 Edward of Woodstock, who took part in the Battle of Winchelsea, is better known by what other name?

Q10 What was Jean Froissart's occupation?

Battle of Minorca

Q1 The Battle of Minorca was fought during what war?

Q2 Who led the Royal Navy during the Battle of Minorca?

Q3 What country did the Royal Navy fight at the Battle of Minorca?

Q4 In what sea was the Battle of Minorca fought?

Q5 What side won the Battle of Minorca?

Q6 Who led the forces of the Royal Navy's opponent at the Battle of Minorca?

Q7 In what year did the Battle of Minorca take place?

Q8 What happened to the Royal Navy's commander after the Battle of Minorca?

Q9 What was the Royal Navy's flagship at the Battle of Minorca?

Q10 The Battle of Minorca led directly to what?

Battle of the Kentish Knock

Q1 The Battle of the Kentish Knock is known by what other name?

Q2 The Battle of the Kentish Knock was fought in what sea?

Q3 Who commanded the Royal Navy at the Battle of Kentish Knock?

Q4 Who commanded the forces of the Royal Navy's opponent at the Battle of Kentish Knock?

Q5 In what year did the Battle of Kentish Knock take place?

Q6 What side won the Battle of Kentish Knock?

Q7 The Royal Navy's commander moved his flag from the *Sovereign of the Seas* to what ship during the Battle of Kentish Knock?

Q8 What was the flagship of the Royal Navy's opponent at the Battle of the Kentish Knock?

Q9 How many days did the Battle of Kentish Knock last?

Q10 The Battle of Kentish Knock was fought during what war?

Ships

HMS *Victory*

Q1 HMS *Victory* is based at what port?

Q2 How many guns does HMS *Victory* have?

Q3 HMS *Victory* is best known for taking part in what 1805 battle?

Q4 In what year was HMS *Victory* launched?

Q5 HMS *Victory* was built at what dockyard?

Q6 In what year was HMS *Victory* moved to a dry dock?

Q7 What rate of ship was HMS *Victory*?

Q8 In what year was HMS *Victory* decommissioned?

Q9 What does HMS *Victory* serve as now?

Q10 HMS *Victory* became whose flagship in 2012?

Golden Hind

Q1 In what century was the *Golden Hind* launched?

Q2 The *Golden Hind* was most famously captained by who?

Q3 What did the *Golden Hind* do between 1577 and 1580?

Q4 What was the *Golden Hind*'s original name?

Q5 The *Golden Hind* was named in whose honour?

Q6 A reconstruction of the *Golden Hind* can be found on what river?

Q7 Who ruled England when the *Golden Hind* was constructed?

Q8 What Spanish galleon did the *Golden Hind* famously capture in 1579?

Q9 In what year was a full-size replica of the *Golden Hind* launched?

Q10 What happened to the *Golden Hind*?

Ark Royal (1587)

Q1 What type of ship was the *Ark Royal*?

Q2 The *Ark Royal* was originally ordered for who?

Q3 What was the *Ark Royal* called before becoming a Royal Navy vessel?

Q4 On what river was the *Ark Royal* built?

Q5 In what river did the *Ark Royal* sink?

Q6 Who ruled England at the time of the *Ark Royal*'s construction?

Q7 What was the *Ark Royal*'s name changed to under James I?

Q8 The *Ark Royal* most famously fought against what fleet?

Q9 The *Ark Royal* was rebuilt at what dockyard in 1608?

Q10 The *Ark Royal* served as whose flagship during the Cádiz expedition of 1625?

HMS *Hood*

Q1 HMS *Hood* was the last of what kind of ship to be built for the Royal Navy?

Q2 What was HMS *Hood*'s pennant number?

Q3 HMS *Hood* was named in whose honour?

Q4 What class of ship was HMS *Hood*?

Q5 In what year was HMS *Hood* launched?

Q6 What shipbuilding company built HMS *Hood*?

Q7 What does HMS *Hood*'s motto *Ventis Secundis* mean?

Q8 HMS *Hood* was sunk during what battle?

Q9 HMS *Hood* served as the flagship of what force for part of the Second World War?

Q10 Who was captain of HMS *Hood* when it was sunk?

HMS *Royal Oak*

Q1 What kind of ship was HMS *Royal Oak*?

Q2 HMS *Royal Oak* was launched during what war?

Q3 HMS *Royal Oak* first saw combat in what battle?

Q4 In what year were HMS *Royal Oak*'s senior officers court martialled?

Q5 HMS *Royal Oak* was sunk by what German submarine?

Q6 What class of ship was HMS *Royal Oak*?

Q7 Where was HMS *Royal Oak* anchored when it was sunk?

Q8 HMS *Royal Oak* was sunk on the outbreak of what war?

Q9 What was HMS *Royal Oak*'s pennant number?

Q10 The wreckage of HMS *Royal Oak* is a designated what?

HMS *Queen Elizabeth*

Q1 What type of ship is HMS *Queen Elizabeth*?

Q2 What record did HMS *Queen Elizabeth* break after being built?

Q3 In what year was HMS *Queen Elizabeth* commissioned?

Q4 What is HMS *Queen Elizabeth*'s home port?

Q5 What is HMS *Queen Elizabeth*'s pennant number?

Q6 What does HMS *Queen Elizabeth*'s motto *Semper Eadem* mean?

Q7 What is the name of the other Queen Elizabeth class ship?

Q8 What was HMS *Queen Elizabeth* named in honour of?

Q9 Who served as the first captain of the HMS *Queen Elizabeth*?

Q10 What type of rose is featured on the HMS *Queen Elizabeth*'s crest?

HMS *Caledonia* (1808)

Q1 How many guns did HMS *Caledonia* have?

Q2 HMS *Caledonia* was launched in what port city?

Q3 HMS *Caledonia* served as whose flagship in the Mediterranean?

Q4 What rate of ship was HMS *Caledonia*?

Q5 In what year did work begin on building HMS *Caledonia*?

Q6 What was HMS *Caledonia* renamed in 1856?

Q7 HMS *Caledonia* was converted to be what kind of ship in 1856?

Q8 In what year was HMS *Caledonia* broken up?

Q9 HMS *Caledonia* participated in the bombardment of what city in 1816?

Q10 Who designed the Caledonia class of ships?

Grace Dieu

Q1 _Grace Dieu_ served as what king's flagship?

Q2 In what year was _Grace Dieu_ launched?

Q3 What happened to _Grace Dieu_?

Q4 Who designed _Grace Dieu_?

Q5 How many voyages is _Grace Dieu_ believed to have embarked on?

Q6 Where was _Grace Dieu_ laid up at the end of its career?

Q7 _Grace Dieu_ was in service until what year?

Q8 _Grace Dieu_ was designed for use against what republic's fleet of carracks?

Q9 What was significant about _Grace Dieu_?

Q10 _Grace Dieu_ set sail in 1420 under the command of the Earl of what?

HMS *Vanguard*

Q1 HMS *Vanguard* was the last of what type of ship to be launched in the world?

Q2 The construction of HMS *Vanguard* began during what war?

Q3 What happened to HMS *Vanguard*?

Q4 What was HMS *Vanguard*'s pennant number?

Q5 What shipbuilder constructed HMS *Vanguard*?

Q6 What was HMS *Vanguard*'s motto?

Q7 In what year was HMS *Vanguard* commissioned?

Q8 Who presided over the HMS *Vanguard*'s launching ceremony?

Q9 Who was HMS *Vanguard*'s first captain?

Q10 HMS *Vanguard* appeared in what *Carry On* film?

HMS *Ark Royal* (1937)

Q1 What type of ship was HMS *Ark Royal*?

Q2 What shipbuilding company constructed HMS *Ark Royal*?

Q3 What does HMS *Ark Royal*'s motto *Desire n'a pas Repos* mean?

Q4 HMS *Ark Royal* was sunk by what German submarine?

Q5 In what year was HMS *Ark Royal* sunk?

Q6 HMS *Ark Royal* was designed to fit the restrictions of what treaty?

Q7 Who was the first captain of HMS *Ark Royal*?

Q8 Who was captain of HMS *Ark Royal* at the time it was sunk?

Q9 In what year was the shipwreck of HMS *Ark Royal* discovered?

Q10 How many crew members died when HMS *Ark Royal* sunk?

HMS *Endeavour*

Q1 HMS *Endeavour* is most commonly associated with what captain?

Q2 What was HMS *Endeavour*'s original name?

Q3 In what year did the Royal Navy acquire HMS *Endeavour*?

Q4 HMS *Endeavour* was scuttled off the coast of what US state?

Q5 In what seaside town was HMS *Endeavour* built?

Q6 What was HMS *Endeavour* renamed after being sold by the Royal Navy in 1775?

Q7 What type of rocket has been named in honour of HMS *Endeavour*?

Q8 The HM Bark *Endeavour* Replica is based at what museum?

Q9 What two countries did HMS *Endeavour* most notably visit on a voyage between 1768 and 1771?

Q10 HMS *Endeavour* was scuttled during what war?

HMS *Warspite*

Q1 What class of ship was HMS *Warspite*?

Q2 In what year was HMS *Warspite* commissioned?

Q3 HMS *Warspite* was decommissioned during what war?

Q4 What does HMS *Warspite*'s motto *Belli dura despicio* mean?

Q5 What was HMS *Warspite*'s nickname?

Q6 What was the first battle that HMS *Warspite* participated in?

Q7 What type of ship was HMS *Warspite*?

Q8 HMS *Warspite* took part in what campaign in the first half of 1940?

Q9 What was HMS *Warspite*'s pennant number?

Q10 How many battle honours did HMS *Warspite* receive?

HMS *Sovereign of the Seas*

Q1 How many guns did HMS *Sovereign of the Seas* have at the time it was launched?

Q2 In what year was HMS *Sovereign of the Seas* launched?

Q3 What rate of ship was HMS *Sovereign of the Seas*?

Q4 During its career, HMS *Sovereign of the Seas* was given what two other names?

Q5 What happened to HMS *Sovereign of the Seas*?

Q6 Who was King of England when HMS *Sovereign of the Seas* was built?

Q7 HMS *Sovereign of the Seas* was launched at what dockyard?

Q8 How many gun decks did HMS *Sovereign of the Seas* have?

Q9 HMS *Sovereign of the Seas* served as whose flagship during the Interregnum?

Q10 What was the first battle HMS *Sovereign of the Seas* took part in?

HMS *Bellerophon*

Q1 What rate of ship was HMS *Bellerophon*?

Q2 How many guns did HMS *Bellerophon* have?

Q3 What was HMS *Bellerophon* renamed?

Q4 HMS *Bellerophon* was converted into what kind of ship in 1815?

Q5 What was HMS *Bellerophon*'s nickname?

Q6 In what year was HMS *Bellerophon* broken up?

Q7 HMS *Bellerophon* served in what two wars?

Q8 Where was HMS *Bellerophon* built?

Q9 Who was the first captain of HMS *Bellerophon*?

Q10 What was the first major battle HMS *Bellerophon* took part in?

HMS *Dreadnought* (1906)

Q1 What type of ship was HMS *Dreadnought*?

Q2 Where was HMS *Dreadnought* built?

Q3 In what year was HMS *Dreadnought* decommissioned?

Q4 What were ships made before HMS *Dreadnought* called?

Q5 Who was the first captain of HMS *Dreadnought*?

Q6 HMS *Dreadnought* was the first capital ship to be powered by what?

Q7 What was HMS *Dreadnought*'s top speed?

Q8 What German submarine did HMS *Dreadnought* sink?

Q9 Why didn't HMS *Dreadnought* take part in the Battle of Jutland?

Q10 Who is credited as the father of HMS *Dreadnought*?

Mary Rose

Q1 *Mary Rose* was built during what English king's reign?

Q2 *Mary Rose* was sunk during what battle?

Q3 In what year was the wreck of *Mary Rose* recovered?

Q4 Where was *Mary Rose* built?

Q5 In what year was *Mary Rose* sunk?

Q6 The remains of *Mary Rose* can be found at what museum?

Q7 In what year was *Mary Rose* substantially rebuilt?

Q8 *Mary Rose* was sunk near what island?

Q9 *Mary Rose* fought its first battle during what war?

Q10 *Mary Rose* served in the Royal Navy for just over how many decades?

HMS *Argus*

Q1 What type of ship was HMS *Argus*?

Q2 What was HMS *Argus* named after?

Q3 HMS *Argus* was built during what war?

Q4 What type of ship was HMS *Argus* originally supposed to be?

Q5 In what year was HMS *Argus* sold for scrap?

Q6 Name one of HMS *Argus*'s nicknames.

Q7 What shipbuilder constructed HMS *Argus*?

Q8 In what year was HMS *Argus* recommissioned?

Q9 What type of ship did HMS *Argus* become in 1944?

Q10 Why was HMS *Argus* placed in reserve for a number of years before being recommissioned?

HMS *Hermes* (1924)

Q1 HMS *Hermes* was the world's first ship to be designed as a what?

Q2 What shipbuilding company built HMS *Hermes*?

Q3 What does HMS *Hermes*'s motto *Altiora Peto* mean?

Q4 In what year was HMS *Hermes* sunk?

Q5 What was HMS *Hermes* named after?

Q6 What was HMS *Hermes*'s pennant number?

Q7 HMS *Hermes* was sunk in what ocean?

Q8 Who was the first captain of HMS *Hermes*?

Q9 HMS *Hermes* served briefly with what fleet at the start of its career?

Q10 HMS *Hermes* was ordered during what war?

Henry Grace à Dieu

Q1 *Henry Grace à Dieu* was known by what other name?

Q2 *Henry Grace à Dieu* served as what king's flagship?

Q3 *Henry Grace à Dieu* was built in response to the construction of what Scottish ship?

Q4 In what year was *Henry Grace à Dieu* commissioned?

Q5 What was *Henry Grace à Dieu* renamed in 1547?

Q6 *Henry Grace à Dieu* was built in what dockyard?

Q7 How many gun decks did *Henry Grace à Dieu* have?

Q8 *Henry Grace à Dieu* took part in what 1545 battle?

Q9 *Henry Grace à Dieu* is believed to have been destroyed by what?

Q10 What happened to *Henry Grace à Dieu* around the year 1536?

HMS *Agamemnon* (1781)

Q1 What rate of ship was HMS *Agamemnon*?

Q2 How many guns did HMS *Agamemnon* have?

Q3 HMS *Agamemnon* is most commonly associated with what Royal Navy hero?

Q4 What was HMS *Agamemnon*'s nickname?

Q5 What shipbuilder built HMS *Agamemnon*?

Q6 What class of ship was HMS *Agamemnon*?

Q7 Who was captain of HMS *Agamemnon* when it sunk?

Q8 HMS *Agamemnon* was wrecked off the coast of what present-day country?

Q9 HMS *Agamemnon* served in what three major wars?

Q10 What is HMS *Agamemnon* named after?

HMS *Bounty*

Q1 HMS *Bounty* was most famously captained by who?

Q2 Who led a mutiny on HMS *Bounty*?

Q3 In what year was HMS *Bounty* launched?

Q4 What happened to HMS *Bounty*?

Q5 What happened to HMS *Bounty* in 1787?

Q6 What was HMS *Bounty*'s original name?

Q7 HMS *Bounty* was built in what port city?

Q8 What was HMS *Bounty* supposed to be acquiring on the voyage where a mutiny famously took place?

Q9 In what year did a mutiny take place on HMS *Bounty*?

Q10 What ship did the Royal Navy dispatch to capture HMS *Bounty*'s mutineers?

Answers

General

General 1 (easy)

Q1 Francis Drake
Q2 HMS *Beagle*
Q3 5
Q4 Calais
Q5 His journal
Q6 New York
Q7 1714
Q8 James Thomson
Q9 Ship worm
Q10 Salt junk

General 2 (easy)

Q1 Physician
Q2 C. S. Forester
Q3 West African Squadron
Q4 1859
Q5 Two-power standard
Q6 40
Q7 5
Q8 Vanguard class
Q9 Admiral
Q10 2005

General 3 (easy)

Q1 Author
Q2 Senior Service
Q3 *Heart of Oak*
Q4 74
Q5 Submarine
Q6 Duke class
Q7 Admiral of the Fleet
Q8 Jack Tar

Q9 Naval slang
Q10 HMS *Dreadnought*

General 4 (easy)

Q1 HMS *Victory*
Q2 Helicopter
Q3 White Ensign
Q4 1901
Q5 Devon
Q6 HMS *Protector*
Q7 5
Q8 USA
Q9 Board game
Q10 First World War

General 5 (easy)

Q1 3
Q2 Plymouth
Q3 Portsmouth
Q4 Slavery
Q5 HMS *Warrior*
Q6 Germany
Q7 Midshipman
Q8 Battle of Trafalgar
Q9 Norman French
Q10 Calais

General 6 (average)

Q1 Her Majesty's Naval Service
Q2 Charles II
Q3 First Sea Lord
Q4 Ministry of Defence
Q5 Kent and Sussex
Q6 English and Scottish Navies
Q7 Horatio Nelson
Q8 Portsmouth

Q9 American Revolutionary War

Q10 First World War and Second World War

General 7 (average)

Q1 Prince Philip, Duke of Edinburgh

Q2 Invergordon Mutiny

Q3 D-Day

Q4 Royal Marines

Q5 Henry VII

Q6 Powerful warship

Q7 *Gloriana*

Q8 Continental Navy

Q9 Iceland

Q10 Falklands War

General 8 (average)

Q1 Tony Radakin

Q2 Flying a flag

Q3 Volunteer Cadet Corps

Q4 Patrick O'Brian

Q5 Second Sea Lord

Q6 Whitehall, London

Q7 HMY *Britannia*

Q8 Edinburgh

Q9 Second World War

Q10 White Star Line

General 9 (average)

Q1 'If you wish for peace, prepare for war'

Q2 Jerry Kyd

Q3 0

Q4 4

Q5 Anglo-Spanish War (1654–1660)

Q6 Commerce raiders

Q7 River Medway

Q8 3

Q9 16th-19th

Q10 2

General 10 (average)

Q1 Invincible class
Q2 Clydebank
Q3 Letter of marque
Q4 Elizabeth I
Q5 Africa
Q6 Battle of Copenhagen
Q7 William Pitt the Younger
Q8 Impressment
Q9 Grand Fleet
Q10 Pre-dreadnought

General 11 (expert)

Q1 Portsmouth, Clyde and Devonport
Q2 Hastings, New Romney, Hythe, Dover and Sandwich
Q3 United Kingdom, France, USA, Italy and Japan
Q4 Rump Parliament
Q5 Third rate
Q6 Sick and Hurt Board
Q7 Zeebrugge Raid
Q8 1914-18
Q9 Somalian pirates
Q10 2010

General 12 (expert)

Q1 John Brown & Company
Q2 *Holyghost de la Tour*
Q3 Line of battle
Q4 HMS *Hercule*
Q5 1808
Q6 1937
Q7 1917
Q8 Jonathon Band

Q9 Rolls-Royce Gnome
Q10 Second World War

General 13 (expert)

Q1 1954
Q2 1797
Q3 Carrack
Q4 Renown class
Q5 1941
Q6 Light cruiser
Q7 1978
Q8 HMS *Cumberland*
Q9 2
Q10 Torpoint, Cornwall

General 14 (expert)

Q1 Royal Scots Navy
Q2 War of the Spanish Succession
Q3 France, Holy Roman Empire and Dutch Republic
Q4 HMS *Albion*
Q5 1936
Q6 Gavin Williamson
Q7 Elizabeth II
Q8 Navy Board
Q9 HMS *Troutbridge*
Q10 Thomas Arne

General 15 (expert)

Q1 'In My Defence God Me Defend'
Q2 6
Q3 Treaty of Utrecht
Q4 Elizabeth II
Q5 Vincent Harris
Q6 Whale Island, Hampshire
Q7 Stone frigate
Q8 Gibraltar Squadron

Q9 Pennant number
Q10 The *Interceptor*

People

Horatio Nelson

Q1 Battle of Trafalgar
Q2 Norfolk
Q3 Midshipman
Q4 HMS *Agamemnon*
Q5 Priest
Q6 Uncle
Q7 Right arm
Q8 Trafalgar Square
Q9 St Paul's Cathedral
Q10 Battle of the Nile

James Cook

Q1 Newfoundland
Q2 Hawaii
Q3 New Zealand
Q4 HMS *Endeavour*
Q5 3
Q6 Kalani'ōpu'u
Q7 1779
Q8 Royal Society
Q9 Elizabeth Batts Cook
Q10 Lono

Harry Paye

Q1 15th
Q2 Privateer
Q3 Owain Glyndŵr
Q4 Poole, Dorset
Q5 Rosemary Manning
Q6 Poole, Dorset
Q7 France and Spain
Q8 Burned it

Q9 His brother
Q10 Kent

Charles Forbes

Q1 Home Fleet
Q2 HMS *Glorious*
Q3 Commander-in-Chief, Plymouth
Q4 Second World War
Q5 Gallipoli campaign
Q6 Queen Alexandra Military Hospital, London
Q7 Norwegian campaign
Q8 Legion of Honour
Q9 HMS *Britannia*
Q10 John Jellicoe

George Rodney

Q1 Battle of the Saintes
Q2 14
Q3 Martinique
Q4 Battle of Cape St. Vincent
Q5 Harrow School
Q6 HMS *Sunderland*
Q7 Brydges
Q8 Fourth Anglo-Dutch War
Q9 Moonlight Battle
Q10 In debt

Edward Hawke

Q1 HMS *Berwick*
Q2 Battle of Quiberon Bay
Q3 Henri-François des Herbiers
Q4 1744
Q5 Plymouth
Q6 First Lord of the Admiralty
Q7 1747
Q8 Barrister

Q9 Sunbury-on-Thames
Q10 Lieutenant

Francis Drake

Q1 Elizabeth I
Q2 New Albion
Q3 *Golden Hind*
Q4 Vice Admiral
Q5 Panama
Q6 Devon
Q7 Thomas Doughty
Q8 Circumnavigate the world
Q9 1581
Q10 Buckland Abbey

Thomas Mathews

Q1 Admiral
Q2 Uncle
Q3 1690
Q4 Wales
Q5 George Byng
Q6 Richard Lestock
Q7 Dismissed
Q8 Rye House Plot
Q9 2
Q10 HMS *Namur*

John Tovey

Q1 Jack
Q2 HMS *Onslow*
Q3 Home Fleet
Q4 Commander-in-Chief, The Nore
Q5 0
Q6 1946
Q7 Baron
Q8 Order of Suvorov

Q9 Durnford School
Q10 Portugal

Walter Raleigh

Q1 Half-brother
Q2 Devon
Q3 James I
Q4 Elizabeth Throckmorton
Q5 Main Plot
Q6 The Lost Colony
Q7 1585
Q8 Beheaded
Q9 Tobacco
Q10 Tower of London

Andrew Cunningham

Q1 Viscount
Q2 ABC
Q3 Dublin
Q4 Mediterranean Fleet
Q5 First Sea Lord
Q6 At sea (near Portsmouth)
Q7 HMS *Scorpion*
Q8 Second Boer War
Q9 Lord High Steward
Q10 First World War

Edward Vernon

Q1 Vice Admiral
Q2 Spain
Q3 Rum diluted with water
Q4 George Washington (Mount Vernon)
Q5 Penryn and Ipswich
Q6 Porto Bello
Q7 Secretary of State for the Northern and Southern Departments
Q8 Westminster

Q9 1700
Q10 Cumberland Bay

Cuthbert Collingwood

Q1 Horatio Nelson
Q2 Newcastle upon Tyne
Q3 HMS *Shannon*
Q4 HMS *Ville de Paris*
Q5 Fareham
Q6 Battle of Trafalgar
Q7 Baron
Q8 12
Q9 HMS *Pelican*
Q10 Cancer

Edward Pellew

Q1 Dover
Q2 Israel Pellew
Q3 50 years
Q4 Viscount
Q5 Falkland Islands
Q6 Matthew Flinders
Q7 Susan Frowde
Q8 Rear Admiral
Q9 Violinist and composer
Q10 HMS *Nymphe*

Charles Beresford

Q1 Conservative
Q2 Nancy Sumner
Q3 Ireland
Q4 1916
Q5 John Fisher
Q6 1874
Q7 5
Q8 Vice Admiral

Q9 HMS *Undaunted*
Q10 HMY *Osborne*

John Jellicoe

Q1 Grand Fleet
Q2 New Zealand
Q3 House of Lords
Q4 St Paul's Cathedral
Q5 1916
Q6 HMS *Camperdown*
Q7 HMS *Britannia*
Q8 Royal Mail Steam Packet Company
Q9 Southampton
Q10 Dreadnought

William Fitzwilliam Owen

Q1 Orphaned
Q2 Rear Admiral
Q3 Canada
Q4 HMS *Culloden*
Q5 Mauritius
Q6 Ontario
Q7 Brother
Q8 Africa
Q9 Chameleon
Q10 American Academy of Arts and Sciences

Alfred Chatfield

Q1 Atlantic Fleet and Mediterranean Fleet
Q2 Coordination of Defence
Q3 Hampshire
Q4 1886
Q5 Commander
Q6 David Beatty
Q7 Baron
Q8 Neville Chamberlain

Q9 HMS *Lion*

Q10 Farnham Common

Barrington Reynolds

Q1 11

Q2 Cornwall

Q3 Rear Admiral

Q4 Slave trade

Q5 Commander

Q6 1857

Q7 Shipwrecked

Q8 Admiral

Q9 9

Q10 St Clement

Edward Howard

Q1 15th

Q2 War of the League of Cambrai

Q3 Norfolk

Q4 Order of the Garter

Q5 France

Q6 *Regent*

Q7 1513

Q8 Henry VIII

Q9 Andrew Barton

Q10 Admiral

Bertram Ramsay

Q1 HMS *Broke*

Q2 Dunkirk evacuation

Q3 Plane crash

Q4 London

Q5 Admiral

Q6 2

Q7 HMS *Crescent*

Q8 Winston Churchill

Q9 1898
Q10 1940

John Leake

Q1 Rochester
Q2 St Dunstan's, Stepney
Q3 First Lord of the Admiralty
Q4 George Rooke
Q5 HMS *Prince*
Q6 Battle of Texel
Q7 Captain
Q8 1
Q9 St Mary's Church in Beddington
Q10 Newfoundland Colony

Baldwin Wake Walker

Q1 Baronet
Q2 Surveyor of the Navy
Q3 Ironclad
Q4 Isle of Man
Q5 Joined the Royal Navy
Q6 Frederic Wake-Walker
Q7 1860
Q8 1
Q9 Morea expedition
Q10 HMS *Queen*

John 'Jackie' Fisher

Q1 2
Q2 Ceylon
Q3 British Army officer
Q4 13
Q5 HMS *Calcutta*
Q6 Commander
Q7 Reforming it
Q8 Frances Katharine Josepha Broughton

Q9 Board of Invention and Research
Q10 Westminster Abbey

Robert Falcon Scott

Q1 *Scott of the Antarctic*
Q2 Ross Ice Shelf
Q3 *Discovery* expedition and *Terra Nova* expedition
Q4 Roald Amundsen
Q5 Kathleen Scott
Q6 13
Q7 Stubbington House School
Q8 43
Q9 Balmoral Castle
Q10 Antarctic fossils

Charles Saunders

Q1 HMS *Gloucester*
Q2 Commander-in-chief
Q3 Western Squadron
Q4 Quebec City
Q5 Westminster Abbey
Q6 War of the Austrian Succession and the Seven Years' War
Q7 Midshipman
Q8 William Pitt the Elder
Q9 James Cook
Q10 Knight of the Bath

Horace Hood

Q1 Rear Admiral
Q2 Battle of Jutland
Q3 1916
Q4 Africa
Q5 Posthumous
Q6 Great-great-grandson
Q7 First
Q8 Joined the Royal Navy

154

Q9 First World War
Q10 HMS *Hyacinth*

John Cabot

Q1 Henry VII
Q2 Giovanni Caboto
Q3 Italy
Q4 15th
Q5 Son
Q6 North America
Q7 Explorer
Q8 Bristol
Q9 St John's
Q10 Place where John Cabot first set foot on North American soil

George Rooke

Q1 1702
Q2 Admiral of the Fleet
Q3 Kent
Q4 William III
Q5 Canterbury
Q6 3
Q7 HMS *London*
Q8 The Netherlands
Q9 Rear Admiral
Q10 France and Spain

Robert FitzRoy

Q1 HMS *Beagle*
Q2 New Zealand
Q3 Ampton Hall
Q4 Suicide
Q5 Vice Admiral
Q6 Charles II
Q7 Half-brother
Q8 Royal Naval Academy

Q9 Tory
Q10 Royal Society

John Jervis

Q1 St Vincent
Q2 3
Q3 Battle of Cape Saint Vincent
Q4 Mediterranean Fleet
Q5 Meaford Hall
Q6 First Lord of the Admiralty
Q7 George Townshend
Q8 Cousin
Q9 Went travelling in Europe
Q10 1799

Augustus Keppel

Q1 Viscount
Q2 Member of Parliament
Q3 Fourth rate
Q4 North America and West Indies Station
Q5 Atlantic Fleet
Q6 Hugh Palliser
Q7 American Revolutionary War
Q8 Whig
Q9 James Cook
Q10 Rear Admiral

William Gonson

Q1 Benjamin Gonson
Q2 Henry VIII
Q3 *Mary Grace*
Q4 10 years
Q5 Norfolk and Suffolk
Q6 Melton Mowbray, Leicestershire
Q7 Treasurer of the Navy
Q8 Merchant and shipbuilder

Q9 Suicide
Q10 Vice Admiral

Samuel Pepys

Q1 A diary
Q2 14
Q3 University of Cambridge
Q4 Jacobitism
Q5 Charles II and James II
Q6 Maid
Q7 Cambridge
Q8 Great Fire of London
Q9 Fleet Street
Q10 70

Roger Keyes

Q1 House of Lords
Q2 Portsmouth North
Q3 India
Q4 Baron
Q5 Army officer
Q6 Conservative
Q7 China
Q8 Leopold III of Belgium
Q9 Combined Operations Headquarters
Q10 Boxer Rebellion

George Byng

Q1 Torrington
Q2 George II
Q3 Southill
Q4 George Rooke
Q5 1718
Q6 Volunteer-per-order
Q7 HMS *Swallow*
Q8 St Paul's, Covent Garden

Q9 Royal Naval Academy
Q10 HMS *Britannia*

Adam Duncan

Q1 Batavian Republic
Q2 1797
Q3 Viscount
Q4 Scotland
Q5 Admiral
Q6 HMS *Trial*
Q7 Naval Gold Medal
Q8 Seven Years' War
Q9 1746
Q10 Commander-in-Chief, North Sea

George Anson

Q1 Jacques-Pierre de Taffanel de la Jonquière
Q2 1747
Q3 Seven Years' War
Q4 3
Q5 Staffordshire
Q6 War of the Spanish Succession
Q7 Moor Park
Q8 Parliament
Q9 1747
Q10 War of Jenkins' Ear

Edward Berry

Q1 Baronet
Q2 HMS *Vanguard*
Q3 HMS *Agamemnon*
Q4 Bath, Somerset
Q5 1806
Q6 Knight Commander of the Order of the Bath
Q7 10
Q8 Uncle

Q9 Lieutenant
Q10 Battle of the Nile

Samuel Hood

Q1 Mediterranean Fleet
Q2 American Revolutionary War
Q3 Vicar
Q4 Joined the Royal Navy
Q5 HMS *Jamaica*
Q6 George Rodney
Q7 Corsica
Q8 91
Q9 France
Q10 Greenwich Hospital

William Cornwallis

Q1 Billy Blue
Q2 Brother
Q3 14
Q4 Admiral
Q5 Eye and Portsmouth
Q6 HMS *Newark*
Q7 0
Q8 French Revolutionary Wars
Q9 HM Yacht *Charlotte*
Q10 1796

James Saumarez

Q1 1801
Q2 Strait of Gibraltar
Q3 France and Spain
Q4 Guernsey
Q5 Admiral
Q6 HMS *Russell*
Q7 French Revolutionary Wars
Q8 Horatio Nelson

Q9 Commander-in-Chief, Plymouth
Q10 Baltic Fleet

Thomas Cochrane

Q1 Napoleon
Q2 Dismissed from the Royal Navy
Q3 4
Q4 1820
Q5 Patrick O'Brian
Q6 Scotland
Q7 A pardon
Q8 Dundonald
Q9 1
Q10 1806

Maurice Suckling

Q1 Uncle
Q2 Captain
Q3 Comptroller of the Navy
Q4 Sister
Q5 Suffolk
Q6 Ordinary seaman
Q7 HMS *Newcastle*
Q8 HMS *Dreadnought*
Q9 Edward Hawke
Q10 13

Frederick Marryat

Q1 Charles Dickens
Q2 *Mr Midshipman Easy*
Q3 *The Children of the New Forest*
Q4 Maritime flag signalling
Q5 Joseph Marryat
Q6 Midshipman
Q7 HMS *Imperieuse*
Q8 *The Metropolitan Magazine*

Q9 To become a fulltime writer
Q10 War of 1812

David Beatty

Q1 Earl
Q2 1st Battlecruiser Squadron
Q3 John Jellicoe
Q4 Washington Naval Treaty
Q5 Cheshire
Q6 Dartmouth
Q7 Alfred, Duke of Saxe-Coburg and Gotha
Q8 First Sea Lord
Q9 Africa
Q10 1927

Dudley Pound

Q1 Isle of Wight
Q2 Battle of Jutland
Q3 1941
Q4 First Sea Lord
Q5 Second World War
Q6 USA
Q7 Barrister
Q8 HMS *Britannia*
Q9 HMS *Repulse*
Q10 Brain tumour

Christopher Cradock

Q1 Battle of Coronel
Q2 Rear Admiral
Q3 HMS *Good Hope*
Q4 *Victoria and Albert II*
Q5 *Sporting Notes from the East*
Q6 Order of the Crown
Q7 Dog
Q8 North Yorkshire

Q9 East Asia Squadron
Q10 Boxer Rebellion

Somerset Gough-Calthorpe

Q1 Fourth Anglo-Ashanti War
Q2 Isle of Wight
Q3 First World War
Q4 1918
Q5 Mediterranean Fleet
Q6 5
Q7 *Bellerophon* class
Q8 1930
Q9 Robert Dunsmuir
Q10 Commander-in-Chief, Portsmouth

Louis Mountbatten

Q1 Burma
Q2 Prince Louis of Battenberg
Q3 Governor General of India
Q4 1955
Q5 House of Lords
Q6 Frogmore House
Q7 University of Cambridge
Q8 Edwina Mountbatten
Q9 Irish Republican Army
Q10 NATO Military Committee

Tom Phillips

Q1 Tom Thumb
Q2 Force Z
Q3 HMS *Prince of Wales*
Q4 Second World War
Q5 Admiral
Q6 Cornwall
Q7 Stubbington House School
Q8 HMS *Campbell*

Q9 Royal Naval College, Greenwich
Q10 He was short

William Parker

Q1 12
Q2 French Revolutionary Wars
Q3 Thomas Parker
Q4 Staffordshire
Q5 2
Q6 Commander-in-Chief, East Indies and China Station
Q7 Lichfield Cathedral
Q8 John Russell
Q9 Retired from the Royal Navy
Q10 Baronet

Francis Harvey

Q1 Battle of Jutland
Q2 HMS *Lion*
Q3 Major
Q4 Kent
Q5 Great-great grandfather
Q6 First World War
Q7 At sea
Q8 Royal Marines
Q9 Admiral
Q10 1892

Cloudesley Shovell

Q1 Scilly naval disaster of 1707
Q2 Nine Years' War
Q3 Rochester
Q4 His maternal grandmother, Lucy Cloudisley
Q5 Cabin boy
Q6 1689
Q7 George Rooke
Q8 Admiral of the Fleet

Q9 John Narborough
Q10 Westminster Abbey

James Somerville

Q1 France
Q2 Force H
Q3 Midshipman
Q4 Admiral of the Fleet
Q5 Wireless officer
Q6 Dinder House
Q7 Commander-in-Chief, Eastern Fleet
Q8 Lord Lieutenant of Somerset
Q9 Granddaughter
Q10 Knight Commander of the Order of the British Empire

Richard Howe

Q1 1794
Q2 Barbados
Q3 HMS *Magnanime*
Q4 American Revolutionary War
Q5 Earl
Q6 London
Q7 Spithead and Nore mutinies
Q8 1782
Q9 Brother
Q10 William Petty and William Pitt the Younger

Robert Blake

Q1 Westminster Abbey
Q2 Parliamentarian (Roundhead)
Q3 South Carolina
Q4 Father of the Royal Navy
Q5 Bridgwater
Q6 New Model Army
Q7 Storming of Bristol
Q8 1649

164

Q9 Second class postage stamp
Q10 Lord Warden of the Cinque Ports

Battles

Battle of Trafalgar

Q1 France and Spain
Q2 1805
Q3 HMS *Victory*
Q4 Pierre-Charles Villeneuve
Q5 William Pitt the Younger
Q6 J. M. W. Turner
Q7 Napoleonic Wars
Q8 Spain
Q9 Cuthbert Collingwood
Q10 27

Battle of Beachy Head

Q1 1690
Q2 Nine Years' War
Q3 France
Q4 English Channel
Q5 1
Q6 Dutch Republic
Q7 William III and Mary II
Q8 Arthur Herbert, Earl of Torrington
Q9 0
Q10 Anne Hilarion de Tourville

Battle of Dogger Bank

Q1 North Sea
Q2 Grand Fleet
Q3 Royal Navy
Q4 First World War
Q5 1915
Q6 David Beatty
Q7 Germany
Q8 Franz von Hipper

Q9 HMS *Lion*
Q10 SMS *Blücher*

Battle of Cape St Vincent

Q1 Anglo-Spanish War (1796–1808)
Q2 John Jervis
Q3 Portugal
Q4 José de Córdoba y Ramos
Q5 1797
Q6 Royal Navy
Q7 HMS *Victory*
Q8 *Nuestra Señora de la Santísima Trinidad*
Q9 130
Q10 Horatio Nelson

First Battle of Cape Finisterre

Q1 George Anson
Q2 War of the Austrian Succession
Q3 Atlantic Ocean
Q4 14
Q5 Jacques-Pierre de Taffanel de la Jonquière
Q6 France
Q7 1747
Q8 HMS *Prince George*
Q9 5
Q10 A convoy

The Glorious First of June

Q1 Atlantic Ocean
Q2 1794
Q3 Richard Howe
Q4 Louis Thomas Villaret de Joyeuse
Q5 *Vengeur du Peuple*
Q6 George III
Q7 Channel Fleet
Q8 Grain

Q9 Atlantic campaign of May 1794
Q10 HMS *Queen Charlotte*

Battle of Jutland

Q1 North Sea
Q2 John Jellicoe
Q3 1916
Q4 High Seas Fleet
Q5 2
Q6 Reinhard Scheer
Q7 Inconclusive
Q8 Grand Fleet
Q9 Break the Royal Navy's blockade on Germany
Q10 First World War

D-Day

Q1 Normandy
Q2 Operation Neptune
Q3 1944
Q4 Operation Bodyguard
Q5 Atlantic Wall
Q6 Utah, Omaha, Gold, Juno, and Sword
Q7 Western Front
Q8 USA
Q9 2
Q10 France

Battle of the Atlantic

Q1 1939-45
Q2 Second World War
Q3 Germany and Italy
Q4 1941
Q5 1941
Q6 3
Q7 Blockade
Q8 German navy

Q9 Battle of the Denmark Strait
Q10 1942

Battle of Scheveningen

Q1 First Anglo-Dutch War
Q2 Commonwealth of England
Q3 Maarten Tromp
Q4 Dutch Republic
Q5 120
Q6 1653
Q7 Netherlands
Q8 Both sides claimed victory
Q9 George Monck
Q10 William Penn

Battle of Lowestoft

Q1 Suffolk
Q2 Second Anglo-Dutch War
Q3 James II
Q4 Jacob van Wassenaer Obdam
Q5 Dutch Republic
Q6 80
Q7 Royal Navy
Q8 1665
Q9 3
Q10 *Eendracht*

Battle of Sluys

Q1 1340
Q2 Edward III
Q3 Hundred Years' War
Q4 Hugues Quiéret and Nicolas Béhuchet
Q5 France
Q6 Battle of l'Ecluse
Q7 Netherlands
Q8 William de Clinton

Q9 River Orwell
Q10 Noble

Raid on the Medway

Q1 Second Anglo-Dutch War
Q2 Prince Rupert of the Rhine
Q3 Dutch Republic
Q4 HMS *Royal Charles*
Q5 1667
Q6 Chatham Dockyard
Q7 6
Q8 Upnor Castle
Q9 Willem Joseph van Ghent and Michiel de Ruyter
Q10 Artist

Battle of San Carlos

Q1 Falklands War
Q2 1982
Q3 5 days
Q4 Royal Navy
Q5 Sandy Woodward
Q6 HMS *Coventry*
Q7 Argentina
Q8 3
Q9 Military Governor of the Falkland Islands
Q10 Margaret Thatcher

Battle of the Nile

Q1 Battle of Aboukir Bay
Q2 1798
Q3 3
Q4 François-Paul Brueys d'Aigalliers
Q5 Horatio Nelson
Q6 *Orient*
Q7 Ottoman Empire
Q8 Horatio Nelson's captains around the time of the Battle of the Nile

Q9 Felicia Hemans
Q10 13

Dunkirk evacuation

Q1 10
Q2 1940
Q3 France
Q4 Operation Dynamo
Q5 300,000 (actually 338,226)
Q6 Battle of France
Q7 'We shall fight on the beaches'
Q8 Gerd von Rundstedt
Q9 Bertram Ramsay
Q10 Merchant vessels

Battle of the Chesapeake

Q1 American Revolutionary War
Q2 Battle of the Virginia Capes
Q3 Thomas Graves
Q4 Atlantic Ocean
Q5 François Joseph Paul de Grasse
Q6 France
Q7 *Ville de Paris*
Q8 HMS *London*
Q9 HMS *Terrible*
Q10 New York

Battle of Quiberon Bay

Q1 France
Q2 Royal Navy
Q3 Seven Years' War
Q4 Edward Hawke
Q5 *Soleil Royal*
Q6 HMS *Royal George*
Q7 Hubert de Brienne
Q8 1759

Q9 1942
Q10 24

Battle of the Saintes

Q1 American Revolutionary War
Q2 4
Q3 George Rodney
Q4 Royal Navy
Q5 Jamaica
Q6 Breaking the line
Q7 West Indies
Q8 1782
Q9 François Joseph Paul de Grasse
Q10 HMS *Formidable*

First Battle of Heligoland Bight

Q1 First World War
Q2 North Sea
Q3 Leberecht Maass
Q4 Royal Navy
Q5 David Beatty
Q6 1914
Q7 1
Q8 0
Q9 1
Q10 Franz von Hipper

Battle of Camperdown

Q1 Adam Duncan
Q2 French Revolutionary War
Q3 North Sea Fleet
Q4 Netherlands
Q5 Jan Willem de Winter
Q6 HMS *Venerable*
Q7 1797
Q8 *Vrijheid*

Q9 Spithead and Nore mutinies
Q10 William Pitt the Younger

Battle of the Falkland Islands

Q1 First World War
Q2 Atlantic Ocean
Q3 German East Asia Squadron
Q4 Doveton Sturdee
Q5 Maximilian von Spee
Q6 1914
Q7 Falkland Islands
Q8 Battlecruiser
Q9 2
Q10 1

The Four Days' Battle

Q1 Second Anglo-Dutch War
Q2 England
Q3 Christopher Myngs and William Berkeley
Q4 Cornelis Evertsen the Elder and Abraham van der Hulst
Q5 1666
Q6 Charles II
Q7 Being one of the longest naval engagements in history
Q8 Dutch Republic
Q9 HMS *Royal James*
Q10 4

First Battle of Algeciras

Q1 James Saumarez
Q2 France and Spain
Q3 French Revolutionary Wars
Q4 1801
Q5 Iberian Peninsula
Q6 6
Q7 HMS *Hannibal*
Q8 Charles-Alexandre Léon Durand Linois

Q9 HMS *Hannibal*
Q10 3

Spanish Armada

Q1 Elizabeth I
Q2 Philip II
Q3 1588
Q4 Charles Howard
Q5 Francis Drake
Q6 Anglo-Spanish War (1585–1604)
Q7 Tilbury
Q8 Spanish Netherlands
Q9 Alonso Pérez de Guzmán
Q10 Plymouth

Second Battle of Cape Finisterre

Q1 War of the Austrian Succession
Q2 Edward Hawke
Q3 Henri-François des Herbiers
Q4 Spain
Q5 1747
Q6 6
Q7 14
Q8 0
Q9 John Moore
Q10 *Tonnant*

Battles of Barfleur and La Hougue

Q1 1692
Q2 Nine Years' War
Q3 France
Q4 Dutch Republic
Q5 Edward Russell
Q6 Anne Hilarion de Tourville
Q7 England and the Dutch Republic
Q8 44

Q9 William III and Mary II
Q10 French invasion of England

Siege of Lyme Regis

Q1 English Civil War
Q2 Royalists (Cavaliers) and Parliamentarians (Roundheads)
Q3 1644
Q4 8
Q5 Dorset
Q6 Bristol
Q7 Maurice of the Palatinate
Q8 Charles I
Q9 Parliamentarians (Roundhead)
Q10 Robert Devereux, Earl of Essex

Battle of Portland

Q1 Three Days' Battle
Q2 First Anglo-Dutch War
Q3 Commonwealth of England
Q4 English Channel
Q5 Maarten Tromp
Q6 1653
Q7 Robert Blake
Q8 Royal Navy
Q9 *Brederode*
Q10 3

Attack on Mers-el-Kébir

Q1 Battle of the Mediterranean
Q2 1940
Q3 France
Q4 Africa
Q5 *Bretagne*
Q6 HMS *Hood*
Q7 *Dunkerque*
Q8 Royal Navy

175

Q9 James Somerville
Q10 Marcel-Bruno Gensoul

Battle of Winchelsea

Q1 1350
Q2 Edward III
Q3 Crown of Castile
Q4 Charles de La Cerda
Q5 Royal Navy
Q6 Hundred Years' War
Q7 English Channel
Q8 'The Spaniards on the Sea'
Q9 The Black Prince
Q10 Chronicler

Battle of Minorca

Q1 Seven Years' War
Q2 John Byng
Q3 France
Q4 Mediterranean Sea
Q5 France
Q6 Roland-Michel Barrin de La Galissonière
Q7 1756
Q8 Executed
Q9 HMS *Royal Katherine*
Q10 Fall of Minorca

Battle of the Kentish Knock

Q1 Battle of the Zealand Approaches
Q2 North Sea
Q3 Robert Blake
Q4 Witte Corneliszoon de With
Q5 1652
Q6 Royal Navy
Q7 HMS *Prince Royal*
Q8 *Brederode*

Q9 1
Q10 First Anglo-Dutch War

Ships

HMS *Victory*

Q1 Portsmouth
Q2 104
Q3 Battle of Trafalgar
Q4 1765
Q5 Chatham Dockyard
Q6 1922
Q7 First rate
Q8 Still commissioned
Q9 Museum
Q10 First Sea Lord

Golden Hind

Q1 16th
Q2 Francis Drake
Q3 Circumnavigated the globe
Q4 *Pelican*
Q5 Christopher Hatton
Q6 River Thames
Q7 Elizabeth I
Q8 *Nuestra Señora de la Concepción*
Q9 1973
Q10 Broken up

Ark Royal (1587)

Q1 Galleon
Q2 Walter Raleigh
Q3 *Ark Raleigh*
Q4 River Thames
Q5 River Medway
Q6 Elizabeth I
Q7 *Anne Royal*
Q8 Spanish Armada

Q9 Woolwich Dockyard
Q10 Edward Cecil

HMS *Hood*

Q1 Battlecruiser
Q2 51
Q3 Samuel Hood
Q4 Admiral class
Q5 1918
Q6 John Brown and Company
Q7 'With favourable winds'
Q8 Battle of the Denmark Strait
Q9 Force H
Q10 Ralph Kerr

HMS *Royal Oak*

Q1 Battleship
Q2 First World War
Q3 Battle of Jutland
Q4 1928
Q5 *U-47*
Q6 Revenge class
Q7 Scapa Flow
Q8 Second World War
Q9 08
Q10 War grave

HMS *Queen Elizabeth*

Q1 Aircraft carrier
Q2 Largest ship in Royal Navy history
Q3 2017
Q4 Her Majesty's Naval Base, Portsmouth
Q5 R08
Q6 'Always the same'
Q7 HMS *Prince of Wales*
Q8 HMS *Queen Elizabeth* (1913), which was in turn named after Elizabeth I

Q9 Jerry Kyd
Q10 Tudor rose

HMS *Caledonia* (1808)

Q1 120
Q2 Plymouth
Q3 Edward Pellew
Q4 First rate
Q5 1805
Q6 HMS *Dreadnought*
Q7 Hospital ship
Q8 1875
Q9 Algiers
Q10 William Rule

Grace Dieu

Q1 Henry V
Q2 1418
Q3 Struck by lightning and burnt
Q4 William Soper
Q5 1
Q6 River Hamble
Q7 1439
Q8 Republic of Genoa
Q9 One of the largest ships of its time
Q10 Devon

HMS *Vanguard*

Q1 Battleship
Q2 Second World War
Q3 Scrapped
Q4 23
Q5 John Brown and Company
Q6 'We lead'
Q7 1946
Q8 Elizabeth II (then Princess Elizabeth)

Q9 William Agnew
Q10 *Carry On Admiral*

HMS *Ark Royal* (1937)

Q1 Aircraft carrier
Q2 Cammell Laird
Q3 'Zeal does not rest'
Q4 *U-81*
Q5 1941
Q6 Washington Naval Treaty
Q7 Arthur Power
Q8 Loben Maund
Q9 2002
Q10 1

HMS *Endeavour*

Q1 James Cook
Q2 Earl of Pembroke
Q3 1768
Q4 Rhode Island
Q5 Whitby
Q6 *Lord Sandwich*
Q7 Space shuttle
Q8 Australian National Maritime Museum, Sydney
Q9 Australia and New Zealand
Q10 American Revolutionary War

HMS *Warspite*

Q1 Queen Elizabeth class
Q2 1915
Q3 Second World War
Q4 'I Despise the Hard Knocks of War'
Q5 Grand Old Lady
Q6 Battle of Jutland
Q7 Battleship
Q8 Norwegian campaign

Q9 03
Q10 15

HMS *Sovereign of the Seas*

Q1 102
Q2 1637
Q3 First rate
Q4 *Sovereign* and *Royal Sovereign*
Q5 Burnt
Q6 Charles I
Q7 Woolwich Dockyard
Q8 3
Q9 Robert Blake
Q10 Battle of the Kentish Knock

HMS *Bellerophon*

Q1 Third rate
Q2 74
Q3 *Captivity*
Q4 Prison ship
Q5 Billy Ruffian
Q6 1836
Q7 French Revolutionary Wars and Napoleonic Wars
Q8 Frindsbury, Kent
Q9 Thomas Pasley
Q10 Glorious First of June

HMS *Dreadnought* (1906)

Q1 Battleship
Q2 Her Majesty's Naval Base, Portsmouth
Q3 1919
Q4 Pre-Dreadnoughts
Q5 Reginald Bacon
Q6 Steam turbines
Q7 21 knots
Q8 SM *U-29*

Q9 Being refitted at the time
Q10 John Fisher

Mary Rose

Q1 Henry VIII
Q2 Battle of the Solent
Q3 1982
Q4 Portsmouth
Q5 1545
Q6 Mary Rose Museum
Q7 1536
Q8 Isle of Wight
Q9 War of the League of Cambrai
Q10 3

HMS *Argus*

Q1 Aircraft carrier
Q2 Argus Panoptes (Greek mythology)
Q3 First World War
Q4 Ocean liner
Q5 1946
Q6 Hat Box or Flatiron
Q7 William Beardmore and Company
Q8 1938
Q9 Accommodation ship
Q10 Budgetary reasons

HMS *Hermes* (1924)

Q1 Aircraft carrier
Q2 Armstrong Whitworth
Q3 'I seek higher things'
Q4 1942
Q5 Greek god Hermes
Q6 95
Q7 Indian Ocean
Q8 Arthur Stopford

Q9 Atlantic Fleet
Q10 First World War

Henry Grace à Dieu

Q1 Great Harry
Q2 Henry VIII
Q3 *Michael*
Q4 1514
Q5 *Edward*
Q6 Woolwich Dockyard
Q7 2
Q8 Battle of the Solent
Q9 Fire
Q10 Remodelled

HMS *Agamemnon* (1781)

Q1 Third rate
Q2 64
Q3 Horatio Nelson
Q4 Eggs–and–Bacon
Q5 Henry Adams
Q6 Ardent class
Q7 Jonas Rose
Q8 Uruguay
Q9 Anglo-French War, French Revolutionary Wars and Napoleonic Wars
Q10 King Agamemnon (Greek mythology)

HMS *Bounty*

Q1 William Bligh
Q2 Fletcher Christian
Q3 1784
Q4 Burned by mutineers
Q5 Sold to Royal Navy
Q6 *Bethia*
Q7 Hull
Q8 Breadfruit

Q9 1789
Q10 HMS *Pandora*

Also by B.R. Egginton

Non-fiction

Shorthand SOS: Learn Teeline shorthand FAST

Henry Hotze: The Master of Confederate Diplomacy

History Essay Writing Basics: For High School and Undergraduate Students

The Ultimate History Quiz

The Ultimate British Prime Ministers Quiz

The Ultimate US Presidents Quiz

The Ultimate English Monarchs Quiz

The Ultimate French Monarchs Quiz

Fiction

A Kingdom of Our Own

The Chronicles of Ascension (composed of six novellas)

The Sixth Number (composed of three parts)

Printed in Great Britain
by Amazon